Nothing in the world smells better than fresh-baked bread. Preston Yancey's words are the book equivalent. These are thoughts to nourish the soul.

JOHN ORTBERG, senior pastor, Menlo Church;
author of *All the Places to Go*

This book is meant to be savored. Slow down, pour a glass of wine, go to your kitchen, pray in the ordinary ways, because you're about to meet with the Holy Spirit in these pages, and you will be changed. It's haunting, lyrical, tactile, and freeing. Preston's book is a homemade altar: gather and lift up your hands.

SARAH BESSEY, author of *Out of Sorts: Making Peace with an Evolving Faith* and *Jesus Feminist*

I will never be a baker of bread. But the way Preston Yancey uses baking bread as an image for our formation in Christ is memorable and profound. There is much wise-heartedness to be received, practiced, and savored here.

SHARON GARLOUGH BROWN, author of *Sensible Shoes: A Story of the Spiritual Journey* and *Two Steps Forward: A Story of Persevering in Hope*

This book will give you two uniquely related gifts—it will make the spiritual disciplines as well as the art of baking bread warmly accessible. From the moment Yancey invites us to pray a blessing over our kitchens—and mine was especially messy that day—we are invited to view the incarnation with fresh eyes. God with us, unembarrassed by the mess that characterizes our lives and profoundly interested in seeing us changed.

In a world where we are held hostage by our own busyness, Yancey reminds us how to be still. How to be intentional. How to knead dough. How to have relationship with a God who is both spirit as well as fully bodied. I am gratefully adding this book to my shelf of cookbooks as a reminder that the daily practice of the spiritual disciplines is as important to the soul as bread is to the body. And just as satisfying.

LISA-JO BAKER, author of *Surprised by Motherhood* and community manager for (in)courage.

Out of the House of Bread is a well-formed, beautifully kneaded, and perfectly timed metaphor, one that led me into a more thoughtful practice of the spiritual disciplines. Never heavy handed, Yancey's words serve as both encouragement for the seasoned practitioner, and instruction to the uninitiated. Simply put, this book is for any soul looking to delve deeper into the spiritual disciplines.

SETH HAINES, author of *Coming Clean*

OUT OF
THE HOUSE
OF BREAD

Also by Preston Yancey

Tables in the Wilderness

OUT OF THE HOUSE OF BREAD

SATISFYING YOUR HUNGER
FOR GOD WITH THE SPIRITUAL DISCIPLINES

PRESTON YANCEY

ZONDERVAN

Out of the House of Bread
Copyright © 2016 by Preston Yancey

This title is also available as a Zondervan ebook. Visit www.zondervan.com/ebooks.

Requests for information should be addressed to:
Zondervan, 3900 *Sparks Dr. SE, Grand Rapids, Michigan 49546*

Library of Congress Cataloging-in-Publication Data

Yancey, Preston, 1989-
  Out of the house of bread : satisfying your hunger for God with the spiritual disciplines / Preston Yancey.
     pages cm
  Includes bibliographical references.
  ISBN 978-0-310-33886-4 (hardcover)—ISBN 978-0-310-33889-5 (ebook) 1.
God (Christianity)—Worship and love. 2. Spiritual formation. 3. Bread—Religious aspects—Christianity. 4. Baking—Miscellanea. I. Title.
BV4817.Y36 2015
  248.4'6—dc23   2015023992

Cover design: James W. Hall IV
Cover photography: © DNY59 / Getty Images®
Interior design: Denise Froehlich
Edited by John Sloan, Bob Hudson, and Becky Jen

First printing November 2015 / Printed in the United States of America

For Dr. David Lyle Jeffrey
and the people of HopePointe Anglican Church,
"In Thy light we shall see light" — Psalm 36:9

Contents

Foreword by Shauna Niequist 11
In the Kitchen: The Path 17
The Recipe 31

IN YOURSELF

Mise en Place: The Examen 39
Measure and Mix: Lectio Divina 51
Kneading: Intercessory Prayer 65

IN THE WORLD

Rising: Wonder 81
Forming: Rootedness 95
Last Form, Last Rise: Remembrance 109

AT THE TABLE

Baking: Fasting 125
Serving: Feasting 137
Setting to Rights: Seasons 151
Commissioning 163

APPENDIXES

Appendix 1: Suggested Resources
        for the Tradition 167
Appendix 2: Suggested Resources
        for Contemplating Icons 171
Acknowledgments 173
Notes 175

Foreword

All my favorite stories are, essentially, stories about God or stories about food, and the very best are stories about both. One of the great losses of modern life and certainly modern faith, it seems to me, is that in many ways we've divorced faith from real, actual life—we've fixed faith firmly in the mind and the heart, respectable places, tidy spots. And then actual life—hands and messes and smells and textures and dirt and bones—those things are just the stuff of the world.

But the world was created, as it were, by divine breath. And it still gasps with divinity, at least to me. For those of us who are listening, the music of faith is being played by those hands and in that dirt and in flour and water, in rocks and trees, in the plain old stuff of life, not simply relegated to the idea realm, tucked away, abstract.

And so then, a book about liturgy and bread baking is totally my jam. Liturgy: the work of the people. The skeleton on which we can hang our words and songs about God. The container that lovingly gathers up our corporate language. And bread: the simplest, most iconic of all nourishment. Bread: the starting point. Bread: one half of the Eucharist feast.

When I first began baking bread, I felt as though I'd all of a sudden gained the ability to perform magic. I'd been an enthusiastic home cook for years but a terrible and uninspired baker. I'm not math-y or precise enough for baking, so I always skip steps, and the results, unsurprisingly, are terrible. What I love about cooking is how live and active it feels, as if the fire and the flavors and I are all talking to each other, responding, adjusting. Baking feels—or felt—like arithmetic, the same every time, a touch boring.

And then I began baking bread, and it felt like a conversation. It felt active and a little different each time. I had to listen and watch, readjust, find warmer or cooler places to let it rise. I had to learn how much kneading was too much and how much too little. And I felt that rush of pleasure when the steam escaped from the first cut. I ate half the first loaf standing at the stove, burning my lips and my fingers, a spoon of cherry jam in one hand, the hot bread in the other.

Chicken, when you cook it, is still chicken. It was raw chicken, and then it becomes cooked chicken. Onions: raw, then cooked. But it's another thing altogether when flour and water and salt and yeast become bread. The closest to magic I've come, I think. And it gets me every time. I take pride in things I make—guacamole or berry crisp or green-chili strata, but the pride I feel about bread baking is something else entirely.

Maybe that pride comes from the transformation, or maybe it comes from the trickiness. I've ruined a lot of things in the kitchen but none so often as bread—it feels as though it has a mind of its own and you're just paying attention. The payoff for the attention is good bread, and it's worth it every time.

And so, of course, with the disciplines of spiritual life: the greatest meaning comes in the trying, the learning, the listening and adjusting. I don't feel I deserve any great reward for those disciplines that come easily to me: truth-telling, connection, hospitality. But the ones that require more from me—Sabbath, silence, solitude? I'm delighted with myself when I manage them, and delighted even more with what they yield in me. As with anything—in the kitchen, in the realm of spirituality—the more one has to struggle for it, the more valuable, the more transformational.

And so a beautiful loaf of bread is a triumph. For me, so is a Sabbath or hard-fought minutes spent in centering prayer, the mind darting less and less often as I practice. With each minute I am able to add to my practice of silence, I feel proud, the same way I did when my first beautiful loaf came from the oven, crackling and steaming.

This is worthwhile work: the spiritual and the culinary both. Partially because work is worthwhile. Our world doesn't reflect that back to us very often these days, but we used to know this, that the best relationships are the ones we've fought for, the deepest truths the ones we've struggled for, the sweetest moments of rest the ones we earned following hard work.

You can buy bread, and you can live a shallow spirituality. Those are easy things to do. Those are the convenient things to do. But the work is an invitation to be transformed, which is what I believe we all really want—more than happiness or comfort.

We want to be transformed, and this beautiful book is one invitation after another to that transformation, through work, through grace, through baking bread and silence and prayer and God's Word. My life has been altered as I've turned the pages, and I believe that kind and intelligent invitation beckons across the pages to you as well.

SHAUNA NIEQUIST,
JUNE 2015

You shall eat in plenty and be satisfied, and praise the Name of the Lord your God, who has dealt wondrously with you.

The eyes of all wait upon you, O Lord: And you give them their food in due season.

O Lord our God, you supply every need of ours according to your great riches: Bless the hands that work in this place, and give us grateful hearts for daily bread; through Jesus Christ our Lord. Amen.

The blessing of a kitchen from the Order of a Celebration of a Home of *The Book of Occasional Services of the Episcopal Church*

In the Kitchen: The Path

⟫⟫⟫⟩ ⟨⟨⟨⟨⟨

I have lived in six kitchens.

One of the more recent ones stood at the end of the world in Scotland, overlooking a roadway and facing a wall of trees that formed a tempestuous wood. In that wood there was a path I would take into town, a walk of about twenty minutes, and for a year I lived my life by relative distance. I was either in town and twenty minutes from home or at home twenty minutes from town. The path itself seemed without time. If after setting out I was called or texted, asked how long I would be, I would say simply, "I'm on the path." The path seemed shorter some mornings and longer some nights, but without fail, a glance at the clock on the way in and again on the way out confirmed a constant: twenty minutes.

This path, with but without time, taught me something of God, about the way we journey in faith. We are on the path but unsure of the distance, though we have some certainty about where we have come from and where we are going. It occurred to me that saying "I'm on the path" may be the truest confession of my faith. It is stripped of self-righteousness, of any surety but this: I am walking forward; I am walking toward. Twenty minutes, or whatever the eternal equivalent might be.

I turned these thoughts over in that kitchen in Scotland, with big French doors and a false balcony at the far end. I would open them on autumn and spring afternoons, and sometimes in the last days of summer when the blue nights were heavy and the sun didn't quite set until midnight. It was in this kitchen, on one end of an existence measured by relative distance, that I learned to bake bread again and learned to fall in love with Jesus again too.

I'm not entirely sure which came first. I suppose that has something to do with saying I'm on the path.

This is a book about being on the path. Or it is a book about being uncertain of how far into the path you are. Or how long you have even been on it. Along the path there are moments of shadow and sunlight, and the path is often at the mercy of the tilt of the earth—the seasons, the rhythms of snowfall and melt and blossom. It is also a book about baking a single loaf of bread and learning a handful of different ways to pray. The ways of praying are often at the mercy of the tilt of the self—the seasons, the rhythms of sorrow and waking and hope.

The bread is the only constant. "I am the bread of life."[1] This is a book about that too.

"What does it mean to be a temple of the Holy Spirit?"

Offhandedly, I ask this to the circle of assembled parishioners when we've all settled into the plush dining-room chairs that have retreated from table to living room. We are a diversity of ages, men and women, bound together by our local church but perhaps not much else. It is the seventh week of our study of a newly drafted Anglican discipleship study, and I remain skeptical that my bishop's request for me to lead this group was a good idea.

I am half the age of the rest of the circle, at least. But I find myself here, facilitating a larger conversation about God.

The question I have unceremoniously dropped like an egg that rolled off a countertop onto a tile floor comes from Paul's first letter to the Corinthians: "Do you not know that your body is a temple of the Holy Spirit within you, whom you have from God?"[2]

We trade responses for a few minutes, hedge our half-answers around certainties about God and Jesus, for we are avoiding too much talk of the Spirit.

The Holy Spirit is the mysterious other of the Trinity, the one no one ever seems to have much familiarity with. And when they do, they are generally not the sorts of people we would invite over for dinner or ask to borrow a pie dish from. (I generally want them to calm down.)

But it is the Spirit, Paul stresses, that dwells within us. Along those lines, I can hear the mysterious words of Saint Athanasius, in the vein of Saint Irenaeus, that "the Son of God became man so that we might become God."[3] In the orthodox Christian tradition this idea is called *theosis*, if you lean East, and *divinization*, if you lean West. Fundamentally, the two words get at the same theological point: we are in process of becoming more and more like Jesus and will in the end be like Jesus.

(You see, the path.)

I share these thoughts with the group, and someone asks if it means we become as God ourselves.

"No," I reply, "it can sound like that's what is being suggested, but the reasoning is a bit more complicated. The Eastern Orthodox Bishop Kallistos Ware describes it by saying Christians are caught up into the being of God. God is like water, all around us, in us too. As God moves, we move.[4] But he goes on to stress this union is limited because we are limited. God may dwell in us, but we are still human. We are not water, but in the water. We can swim, we can drink the water in, the water is in us and gives us life, but we are not the water."

"So is that what it means to be a temple of the Holy Spirit?" someone refrains. "Does it mean to be drowning in the waters of God?"

Does it mean that?

"And God said, Let us make man in our image, after our likeness."[5]

There is a pear-and-blackberry cobbler with cherry-and-bourbon-ginger syrup and an almond crust in my oven right now.

Almond meal is tricky to work with, prone to stickiness when fat and liquid have been cut into it, unforgiving in keeping its shape unless first chilled. It makes me think of image and likeness from dust and breath of God. God takes the dirt God has created and mounds it, shapes it, then breathes deep inside to make man. The breath, the very animation of our limbs, comes from God. The breath like the water, giving us our inheritance as unique in creation, made in God's image and likeness.

We take the belief of the *imago Dei*, being made in the image of God, from the first chapter of Genesis. It is the assurance of the uniqueness of our creation. It is a common phrase, shared across denominational lines. In popular religious speak the *imago Dei* has become little more than a casual aside, something children might hear in Sunday school. They are told we are made in God's image, which too often leaves them thinking God must have hands and feet like theirs, be white or blond or blue-eyed. The Almighty is reduced to a non-triune god that shares more in appearance with Coca-Cola's Santa Claus than anyone from the ancient Near East.

(For this reason, I have made the effort in this book to not use gendered pronouns in reference to God unless referring specifically to Jesus. Jesus is the only person of the Trinity whose gender has been made known to us in the incarnation. Faithful Christians have noted that since God is spirit, as Jesus testifies, and God the Father and God the Holy Spirit do not have physical human bodies, gendered language can be a hindrance to our full engagement with who God is. If we are truly made in the image and likeness of God, that image and that likeness are not gendered but shared across genders.)

Writers in the early church felt it necessary not only to emphasize the mystery of the *imago Dei* but also the distinction between image and likeness. Origen says something to the effect that God's image and likeness are distinct in us.[6] The image is what we all have by nature of being created, but the likeness of God was lost to us in the fall. When sin entered the world, the likeness of God was tarnished, obscured; we do not look as God in our thought, word, and deed—we look as sinful humans. We have the capacity to be like God because of the image in us, but we are hindered by our tarnished likeness.

The tricky work of almond meal is its sticky and unforgiving formation into what it is meant to become. Of the dust God made us— *is making us*—is still making us into what we are meant to become, though we too are sticky, unforgiving in our formation.

After the fall, God did not walk with humankind in the intimacy once enjoyed in Eden. It would take an ongoing relationship with an itinerant shepherd named Abram and his descendants for the unity of God and us all to be restored. This is the story we know: the people of Israel, the coming of Jesus.

But let's linger a moment. Let's take the path slow and see what we might find.

The book of Exodus is a curious book of the Bible. While Greek Christians named it after the triumphant freeing of the Israelites from their slavery in Egypt, led by Moses and Aaron through the power of God, into the wilderness to seek the Promised Land, only half of the book focuses on the exodus itself. The original Hebrew name of the book is *Sh'mot*, Names. This makes a bit more sense, because the second half of the book is devoted to the building of the tabernacle, the tent where God says God will dwell with the people, be present with and to them. Verse after verse details specifics regarding the decoration and construction of the holy tent, the quality of the craftsmanship and attention to be paid in its construction and all that will be found inside. Thus, Names reminds us that the people brought out of Egypt in the exodus were once a people without name, but have now been called the children of God. They receive this title in full when they worship God, when God is in the midst of them. Their name is connected beyond their deliverance—it says whose they are.

The narrative of the tabernacle building begins after Moses has led the people out into the wilderness. There is an expectation, perhaps even in the text itself, Moses will be the one asked to build the tabernacle. God, however, instructs him otherwise:

> The Lord said to Moses, "See, I have called by name Bezalel the son of Uri, son of Hur, of the tribe of Judah, and I have filled him with the Spirit of God, with ability and intelligence, with knowledge and all craftsmanship, to devise artistic designs, to work in gold, silver, and bronze, in cutting stones for setting, and in carving wood, to work in every craft.... And I have given to all able men ability, that they may make all that I have commanded you ... According to all that I have commanded you, they shall do."[7]

God has a particular person in mind for building the tabernacle: Bezalel; indeed, God calls specific people from Israel who are particularly skilled to create the objects that will go in the tabernacle itself.[8]

What makes these people so special? Is it simply they are more skilled? More artistic?

In the above passage, the ESV has translated *skill*, but the word in the Hebrew transliterated *chakam-leb*, translates literally as *wise-hearted*. God says it is the wise-hearted—not the skilled—who will build the tabernacle, the place where God's glory will dwell with Israel. (Not incidentally, what God describes in Deuteronomy as the place where God "will cause [God's] Name to dwell."[9]) In Exodus 35 and 36, we see again all those who are to work on the tabernacle, men and women alike, are described as wise-hearted.[10]

According to Exodus, these wise-hearted people also build the Ark of the Covenant.[11] The ark is effectively the seat upon which God comes and rests to rule over the people, to be in fellowship with them, but because of God's awesome holiness, the people are hidden from God behind a veil in the tabernacle. The tabernacle is the place where God is found, the ark the place where God's presence chooses to dwell. Through many vast wildernesses the tabernacle endures, the movable tent sheltering the presence of God traveling with Israel wherever it went. Though there were times God made God's own self known outside of the sacred tent, the ark housed within the tabernacle was the place where God had vowed to be found. If the people should seek God there, God would answer.

Centuries after the tabernacle was constructed, the Israelites had settled and established the kingdom of Jerusalem. No longer did they move about the wilderness, so they felt compelled to establish for God a permanent home. King David went into the presence of the Lord and asked to build a temple for the ark. But God replied this was not for David to do. It would be the work of one of David's children, Solomon. In 1 Kings we read that Solomon loved the Lord and God granted him the right to ask for whatever he wished. Solomon asked for wisdom, to which God replied:

> Because you have asked this, and have not asked for yourself long life or riches or the life of your enemies, but have asked for yourself

understanding to discern what is right, behold, I now do according to your word. Behold, I give you a wise and discerning mind, so that none like you has been before you and none like you shall arise after you.[12]

Again, our translations don't quite grasp it. In 1 Kings, Solomon asks God for the Hebrew word *chakam, wisdom*, but God replies with such approving of this desire that God gives Solomon something even better: *chakam-leb, wise-heartedness*.

Once more, the person responsible for building a place where God will reside with the people is explicitly said to be wise-hearted. The medieval rabbinic scholar Rabbi Shlomo Yitzchaki writes: "A person does not request [wise-heartedness] unless he has the fear of Heaven in his heart, as it is stated (Ex. 18:21): 'But you must seek out from the people men of ability, God-fearing men.'"[13] *God-fearing* is another way of translating *wise-hearted*. Here, Rashi has noted what Solomon is being given is the same as what was given to those who were to build the tabernacle.

In the Old Testament, only a few people were said to have this quality. Only to a few was the honor given. But we know as Christians the Spirit of God is within us, and if the Spirit is within us, truly within us, then what could that mean for our own requests to have wisdom?

Can we ask to be wise-hearted too? I think we can.

I think that's also something to do with being on the path.

In 587 BC, the Babylonians destroyed the temple Solomon had built and took the Israelites as captives into Babylon. There is no record of what happened to the ark, though speculation ranges from its seizure by the invaders to God miraculously hiding it until its revelation at the end of all things. Regardless, the place where God had promised God's presence and the place where God's presence had been housed were lost to the people of God. When they returned in 538 BC, they began a just-over-twenty-year project building a new temple, but one that did not have the ark within it. This time, the temple did not house the presence of God.

We date Malachi's prophetic work around this time, the last prophet of Israel. For this reason, Protestants hold no Scripture was written after Malachi before the New Testament. God was no longer present to the people, who lived in the silence of God for hundreds of years. We call this the intertestamental period, during which the Jews were conquered by Greek-speakers and needed a way to preserve the Hebrew Bible. Jewish scholars together created the translation of the Scriptures into Greek called the Septuagint, often-abbreviated LXX, the Seventy, so-called for the number of scholars legend holds were a part of the translation.

The LXX contains, in addition to the Old Testament, a handful of books we call the Apocrypha. The Apocrypha is not considered Scripture by Protestant believers but is a reflection of what faithful Jews were thinking about during the period of silence when God did not speak through prophets. Over the centuries, orthodox Christians have used the Apocrypha as they would any other text written by a saint in the church: as helpful for revealing truths about God but not the Truth of God on their own.

In one of the books of the Apocrypha, the Wisdom of Solomon, we read:

> God of my ancestors, merciful Lord, by your word you created everything. By your Wisdom you made us humans to rule all creation, to govern the world with holiness and righteousness, to administer justice with integrity. Give me the Wisdom that sits beside your throne; give me a place among your children.[14]

Wisdom.

Wisdom that directs and guides. Wisdom, if we are mindful of it, that must be the same kind of wisdom that those who were called wise-hearted had. Writers in the early church found this description of wisdom to be foreshadowing Jesus. In fact, for centuries it was common practice to read this passage during Christmas Vigil, just before the gospel account of the birth of our Lord. The wisdom of God, which does all God's good purposes and work, must be what those who were wise-hearted had within them.

This, or something akin to it, is what it means to be caught up in the life of God. At the very least, what it means to be made not just in the image of God, but in the likeness of God.

In John 1 we read: *And the Word became flesh and dwelt among us, and we have seen his glory, glory as of the only Son from the Father, full of grace and truth.*[15]

The Word became flesh and *dwelt* among us. In the Greek, the word *dwelt* is more closely translated *pitched his tent*. He pitched his tent among us. When the Old Testament was translated into Greek for the LXX, the same phrasing was used to describe God's dwelling within the tabernacle. It was in there God had pitched God's tent among us, in our midst. Stretching across hundreds of years of stories and history, we find Jesus does not merely come and dwell with us. Jesus becomes flesh, becomes the ark of God's presence once more, and *tabernacles* with us. God comes and makes a human body the place where we come to meet God. No longer do we meet God in the tent of a tabernacle or the great stone structure of a temple. In the person of Jesus Christ God is right here, the ark walking around, in our midst.

You have heard this before, you have read it before, but linger a moment on the point. So often we rush to the cross, to the resurrection, and we miss the terrible and awesome moment that is the incarnation. The infinite God comes to dwell personally and finitely in our midst. God has hands, God has feet, but these hands and feet do not stretch across the sky like a cosmic Santa; these hands and feet pick up little children and hold them close, cover blind eyes with spit and mud and make them see, stretch deep across a tree, twist inward to hold a weeping sister.

God, very God, with us completely. But only for a little while. We know this story. Jesus will ascend into heaven. Jesus will no longer be with us in a physical sense. The God who is with us, who tabernacles with us, temples with us, is also taken back beyond our reach.

That cobbler in the oven. I am thinking about God forming us like almond meal. I am thinking about how much we do not want to be changed. How much we do.

"So what?" Someone in the circle asks this earnestly. "We know this part: Jesus is gone; now we just wait around. What does any of this tabernacle and temple stuff have to do with that? We may as well be a people without a God."

Pentecost is the answer to what would otherwise be a people without a God. At his ascension, Jesus promises he will send the Holy Spirit, who will give power and authority to all the disciples, men and women alike, who are present and who are yet to come. It's a sobering declaration when we have spent so much time over the course of Scripture reading about the special people called by God to create the spaces where God would dwell, those who longed for the wisdom of God to come down to them and lead them, who have been with the Jesus who tabernacled among them. Now God says there is but one more thing.

I smile around the circle, "We're coming right back to the beginning, right back to that image and likeness business. We know well what the image is, even though it is beyond us, but we know so little of the likeness, of becoming more and more like God. God has made a way, though."

Pentecost is the linchpin, the thing on which this great cosmic mystery hinges. At Pentecost and ever since, every person who has called on the name of the Lord Jesus and is saved by him is also given the Holy Spirit, alive and full within them. The Spirit comes and dwells. The presence of God dwells within us. We become tabernacles, the ark within us in a spiritual sense as the ark was in Mama Mary, who brought Jesus into the world. We too are bringing Jesus into the world. For this reason Paul poses his question in the first place, asking the Corinthians if they remember they were made temples of God.

Paul would have used the LXX as his Scripture because he was a Greek-speaking Jew. He would have been familiar with the words used to describe the tabernacle, what it would mean to be called wise-hearted, what was written in the Book of Wisdom. Knowing all this, is it any wonder Paul writes: *We preach Christ crucified, a stumbling block to Jews and folly to Gentiles, but to those who are called, both Jews and Greeks, Christ the power of God and the wisdom of God.*[16]

Christ, the power and wisdom of God. The wisdom of God. The pieces weave together, almond meal relenting into shape. By what power is Jesus within us? The Holy Spirit. And who is this Jesus? Very God, the wisdom of God. I'm reminded of the phrases of my evangelical youth. Are we not saying someone is a temple of the Holy Spirit when we say they have asked Jesus to live in their hearts? What's more, if Jesus is the wisdom of God, then are we not also saying the person is wise-hearted? Are we not suggesting God has made a way for every person who calls on God's name to become wise-hearted themselves? A people uniquely gifted and skilled to create and build the places in which God comes to dwell and rest with them? Wise-hearted is the descriptor used in the Old Testament for those who made places for God to dwell on the earth.

I look around the circle of people I sit with. "You and I, now— right now—are called wise-hearted. Jesus is within us, and we are all able to make places where God is glorified and made known in the world. Paul is saying you and I are the living, breathing, walking-around places where God's presence dwells and is made known and we better start taking that seriously." I turn and look to each: "You are a temple of the Holy Spirit. You are a tabernacle. You, in your very limbs, in your very body, are the place where God is present. The image. The likeness. God is not so far from each of us after all."

If we are temples of the Holy Spirit, then the likeness of God in us is being ever-refined. Paul says as much to the Romans, about the Spirit in us praying in all the ways we forget or don't know how to. Jesus in us is constantly polishing the darkened mirror of our souls that is to reflect his glory, a glory we share in with him. But we get tired and weary of the process, reach for tools to help along the way. This is when most of us pick up the next study guide or the next 90-day Bible-reading plan and make valiant attempts to do, do, do in order to feel something of holiness. There's nothing wrong with those study guides, those reading plans, except when we leverage them as means to an end and not as expressions of a relationship we long to deepen. We are never finished with being a Christian, so the next new study, the next new trend, satisfies for a time and then there is more to want, to learn, to discover. This is a gift but it can be exhausting. This too is about the path. This too is about the baking of bread. The path and the baking of bread can teach us something about the long haul of faithfulness, the tireless work of the easy yolk of Jesus.

This is a book about prayer as a kind of open-ended doing. In the doing you meet God. In the doing you meet yourself. But the doing doesn't have defined ends beyond that.

Over the course of this work, we will journey through the making of a single loaf of bread and the practice of several different kinds of prayer called spiritual disciplines. Spiritual disciplines are like a well-stocked chocolate drawer. You never know what you might need at a given time, but the security of knowing you have plenty on hand and having just enough when you need it is vital. Spiritual disciplines are kinds of prayer, and when you find yourself in the middle of a season where nothing spiritual seems to matter and nothing feels like it's working, having something new to try, a different perspective, a new way of telling God you're in need or you're lonely or you're just fed up can feel like a lifeline. It can be a lifeline.

Some of the disciplines in this book would be called classics, some are gently reinterpreted, some are just barely brushing the surface of deep wells of tradition. Think of this work as an invitation, not a crash course. Gently and patiently let us go this path. I can make no promises you will like every practice, but I can assure you there will be one or two you won't. All I ask is that you try each. Give it a go. Give it your all. Dare God to meet you in the midst of what feels ridiculous or in the midst of what feels like you've been doing for years.

And bake some bread. We're going to be baking a lot of bread, a lot of the same bread. The reason is the practice of baking is, to me, less about following a recipe than it is learning the feel of dough and how the humidity of a room changes the texture of the crust. Bit by bit we'll talk about things like that, talk about how being present and focused in the making of this bread is a lot like being intent and focused in prayer. We'll practice a lot, we'll "bake it out," as I say often, and in this practicing you'll feel rooted to so many of the basics you can glide into more challenging and more diverse recipes afterward without hesitation.

While there's no right way to go through this book, it's structured assuming you will progress through it in order, giving each chapter a week. I would suggest you read one chapter, try your hand at a loaf of bread for the week, and try your hand at a spiritual discipline in tandem. The following week, bake a new loaf of bread, begin a new spiritual practice.

By the end, you should have enough practices—nine—and bread—one really fine practiced loaf—to feed yourself and those in your life during the lean times, the times of plenty, and the seasons between. The recipe on pages 31–36 is detailed enough so that you can go ahead and begin right now, today, with each chapter giving a bit more detail and insight to specific parts of baking along the way. You'll also find a gluten-free option back with the general recipe. (The general recipe, with gluten, is already vegan.) The theological significance of dough forming is not lost on you, should you be making the gluten-free loaf. Follow along the chapters all the same. Bake some bread and invite a friend or two over and ask them what they've dared God to do lately. (Always a safe question when someone has just poured the wine and your hands are submerged in yeasty flour.) Find out where they are on the path.

Because hear me: it's a long short stretch into eternity. It's better to not go alone.

Unto us a child is born. Jesus, holy God become wholly human in a manger in a town called Bethlehem, which means House of Bread. Out of the House of Bread our Savior comes, comes as we are, comes as we might be, sent, too, out of that house, out into this world.

I have lived in six kitchens.

In three out of the six kitchens I have called home, I have prayed a blessing over the space before any great work—moving in, moving out, holiday feasts. Under the great umbrella of orthodox Christian faith, I am an Anglican by creed. Anglicans, along with many other liturgical denominations, believe in the blessing of spaces. Like tabernacles and temples long ago, we believe that consecrating spaces unto God is important, that prayer gets into the bones of a place, the brick and mortar.

I am going to ask you to do the thing that sounds both ridiculous and ordinary all at once: go to your kitchen and pray.

This is a book about prayer that is bodied. Prayer that has movement. Prayer that has meat to it. Prayer that has power because the very Spirit of God dwells in you and is polishing you up, with your participation, into the full likeness of Jesus Christ. Though the early church writer Origen reminds us this will not be complete until eternity, the practice of seeking it is the very bringing forth of the kingdom of God, God's presence in the world, that each and every one of us as believers has been called to do.

Right now, walk into your kitchen and lift up your hands to God and pray, eyes open and out loud, that God will show up right there in the midst of you while you bake. It doesn't matter if it looks all picked up and pristine or a total disaster. The mess is holy and so is the uncluttered.

Pray that God will best you. Pray that God will comfort-laugh-shout-sing-over you. Pray until there's no more breath in your lungs. Pray until your whisper becomes a shout or your shout a whisper. And when it's all said out, when the asking of God to be near and present and with is all spent, get quiet. Stand there arms out and eyes open and just breathe. Stand before and in the midst of God and take a breath that is so deep it roots you to the very earth beneath you; then let it go, give it back to God.

Now let's begin.

The Recipe

This recipe, with its many names and iterations along the same central theme, comes from years of use and a variety of sources. I think it was originally adapted from the recommendation of King Arthur flour, of which the late Raymond Calvel, known in France as "the Godfather of Bread," wrote that of all the flours he had tasted in the United States, it came closest to what he used in his homeland. Then came several years of adjustment, a few new techniques thanks to some advice from one or two friends, and then Constance's guidance, as you'll read, when I learned to *feel* bread more than I measured it. This is the result.

Makes 2 loaves.

Total time is about six hours, though only a fourth of that requires your direct involvement. You're waiting the rest of the time.

INGREDIENTS

scant 8¼ cups plus ½ cup unbleached all-purpose flour
3 cups very warm water, nearly hot, divided into 2¾ cup and ¼ cup
7g, or 1 packet, active dry yeast
1 tablespoon raw sugar
1 teaspoon honey
1 tablespoon plus 1 teaspoon salt, finely ground or table
a neutral oil, like vegetable or grape seed

SPECIAL SUPPLIES

dough knife or serrated knife

pastry scrape (referred to in some chapters, for convenience
but not necessary)

two 8" bannetons — or two 8" bowls are just fine

two large, thin kitchen towels, like flour sack, which
will be dusted with flour

a Dutch oven or French oven; if not, the recipe accommodates
with a baking sheet and casserole dish

TO MAKE

1. Begin by ensuring all ingredients are accounted for, that is,
   perform a *mise en place*. (Read through this whole recipe, make
   sure you have everything you need, then keep going.)

2. In a small bowl — I use a Tupperware with a lid — pour ¼ cup
   very warm water over yeast, sugar, and honey. Let steep and
   melt for fifteen minutes. During this time, in a large bowl, mix
   together 8¼ cups flour and the 2¾ cups of the remaining very
   warm water, mixing with a spoon or your hands until a shaggy
   but eventually sleek dough forms. Leave this to rest, covered on
   the counter with a kitchen towel, for about fifteen minutes.

3. Add salt to the dough — I crush mine with a mortar and pestle
   before I do. Mix the yeasty sugar solution, either with a whisk
   or by covering the container with a lid and giving it a good
   shake, then pour it over the dough, kneading a bit in the bowl
   until the liquid and salt begin to be incorporated and the dough
   is smooth.

4. Turn the dough out onto a very lightly floured surface to knead,
   using the flour from your remaining ½ cup. Knead by folding
   the far edge of the dough back over on itself toward you. Press
   into the dough with the heels of your hands and push away.
   After each push, rotate the dough 90°. Repeat this process in

a rhythmic, rocking motion for about five to seven minutes, sprinkling only enough additional flour over the surface where you are kneading to keep the dough from sticking. Along the way, you will feel the dough loses stickiness and turns supple. Not hard, but firm and smooth. The dough should be slightly elastic, bouncing back slowly when you press your finger against it to indent its surface.

5. Coat a bowl with neutral oil in its base and along its sides, as well as your hands. Transfer the dough to the bowl. Cover the bowl with plastic wrap and leave to sit in a warm place for thirty minutes, then uncover it, fold the dough in half, and re-cover it. Leave to rise another hour and a half.

6. At this point, the dough will have risen by a good half its original size. Carefully transfer the dough back to where you kneaded it and, using a dough knife, cut the dough in half, then shape into two smaller rounds. Dust the tops with flour and loosely cover with a kitchen towel and leave to rest for fifteen minutes.

7. Once more, shape the dough into rounds. Fold it under itself until smooth all around except its bottom, where the seam cozily hides. Leave to rest five minutes while you prepare two bread bowls—while this is detailed in the chapter "Last Form, Last Rise: Remembrance," using two similar-sized bowls about 8" in diameter is just fine—lined with kitchen towels that have no fuzz or lint and that have been well-dusted with flour. Transfer the dough seam-side up into these bowls and then fold over the towels. Put them into the fridge until nearly doubled in bulk, about an hour to an hour and a half.

8. If using a Dutch or French oven: Place your Dutch oven, lid on, on the bottom rack of your oven and preheat it to 500F. Pull one loaf from the fridge and tip it, now smoothed seam-side down into the blazing hot Dutch oven. Quickly slash the top of the loaf three or more times diagonally, then spritz well with

cold water to improve the crust. Put the lid back on and return to the hot oven to bake for fifteen minutes. Then, reduce the heat to 450F and bake fifteen minutes more. Then, remove the Dutch oven lid and bake for fifteen minutes uncovered or until very golden brown, about thirteen minutes in my oven, maybe even up to twenty in yours.

9. If not using a Dutch oven, prepare your oven by placing a roasting pan full of boiling water on the bottom rack of a cold oven. Then, preheat the oven to 500F for fifteen minutes. Prepare loaves as above, but on a baking sheet, then slide into the oven to bake for fifteen minutes. Lower the temperature to 400F and bake for twenty more minutes. Test loaves by flicking their bottoms. If it sounds hollow, they are done; if not, return to bake an additional ten minutes and check again.

10. Remove the bread from the oven and place the loaf on a wire rack to cool for at least an hour before cutting to preserve moisture and allow the crust to soften into crispy delight. In the meantime, return the Dutch oven, covered, to the oven and the heat back to 500F. Let preheat, then sit for ten minutes more before repeating as with the first loaf.

As Above, but Gluten Free

When I lived in Scotland, I had a standing tradition of inviting anyone who wished over for dinner on Sundays. This made things a bit tricky when it came to food allergies and preferences. We juggled, learned sensitivities, convinced one or two people to try octopus, and converted one or three or five to a deep appreciation of the diversity of hot peppers in the world, their variant powers and charms.

One of the consistent challenges was the gluten-free needs of some, because baking is only recently trying to do right by people who are gluten intolerant. Most of our traditional recipes are not designed to adapt, and substitutions are often left wanting. I am convinced, though, that it is possible if one is persistent.

This sandwich loaf, everyday loaf, whatever-you-want-to-call-it loaf is one of the best I've ever made, and it owes thanks to a handful of sources: King Arthur flour; some general recommendations and tips from Joy Wilson, a.k.a. Joy the Baker, and Tracy Benjamin, a.k.a. Shutterbean; and, importantly, to Lauren Bently, who tried all the versions of gluten-free things I attempted during the year she and her wonderful husband spent having Sunday dinners in my kitchen, and who was not afraid to tell me what did and did not work.

INGREDIENTS

3 cups King Arthur Gluten-Free Multi-Purpose Flour, or make
    your own brown rice flour blend, described below
2 tablespoons sugar
1 tablespoon honey
2 teaspoons instant yeast
1¼ teaspoons salt
1¼ teaspoons xanthan gum
1 cup warm whole milk
4 tablespoons soft unsalted butter, best quality
3 large eggs

TO MAKE

1. Place the flour or flour blend, sugar, honey, yeast, salt, and xanthan gum in a bowl or the bowl of your stand mixer and mix till combined. Gluten-free bread is not forgiving in terms of blending, so go ahead and use an electric mixer, either hand or stand, for this process.

2. While you continue to beat the mixture, drizzle in the milk. At first, the dough mixture will be crumbly but will combine as the milk is added.

3. To this, add the butter and beat until thoroughly blended.

4. Adding them one at a time, beat in the eggs, thoroughly beating after each addition before adding another. To ensure it is all combined, scrape the bottom and sides of the bowl, then beat

at high speed for three minutes until you have a smooth, thick batter.

5. Cover the bowl, leaving the batter to rise for one hour.

6. Carefully scrape down the bottom and sides of the bowl, gently deflating the batter in the process.

7. Grease an 8½" x 4½" loaf pan, or a 9" x 4" x 4" *pain de mie* pan.

8. Scoop the dough into the pan. Press it level, using a spatula or your wet fingers. I prefer the spatula, not because of mess, but I find it easier to smooth.

9. Cover with greased plastic wrap, and set in a warm place to rise until the loaf barely crowns above the rim of the 8½" x 4½" pan; or till it comes to within about an inch of the rim of the 9" *pain de mie* pan, about forty-five to sixty minutes. Toward the end of the rising time, preheat the oven to 350F.

10. Bake the bread for thirty-eight to forty-two minutes, until golden brown. If you're using a *pain de mie* pan, leave the lid on the entire time. Remove the bread from the oven, turn it out of the pan, and cool on a rack. Then feast.

BROWN RICE FLOUR BLEND

Combine 6 cups stabilized brown rice flour with 2 cups potato starch and 1 cup tapioca flour or tapioca starch. The mixture should be stored in an airtight container at room temperature. King Arthur notes that you can substitute white rice flour for the brown rice flour if you like, but cautions that it'll make your baked goods grittier. I recommend the brown rice both to remove grit and because of its soft sweetness. The blend should keep up to six months.

In Yourself

In the first three weeks, we consider disciplines focused on cultivating awareness of ourselves in relation to God.

. We will first explore how the Spirit teaches us who we are, then how the Scripture teaches us who we are, and, finally, how God relates to who we are.

Here is where we begin, wanderers on this path. We begin in ourselves, where the soil is fertile, where the work is most needed.

Mise en Place: The Examen

$\Longrightarrow\!\!\!\Longrightarrow\!\!\!\Longrightarrow$ —— $\Longleftarrow\!\!\!\Longleftarrow\!\!\!\Longleftarrow$

Mise en place is a French term shared between professional and home kitchens. In the professional setting, it refers to all the dishes and ingredients being prepared in advance for the night's dinner service. In the home kitchen, particularly when referenced in baking, it refers to having everything out, in order, and ready before you begin. If the recipe calls for room-temperature butter or eggs, they have already been set out in preparation. If a bowl is to be chilled, a double broiler put into service, a rolling pin called upon, they have been stationed accordingly. *Mise en place* requires the careful reading of a recipe, often a few times, to ensure not only all ingredients and equipment are on hand but also the baker is anticipating their use. There's nothing worse than realizing an oven should have been preheated or a special pot required when you're already six steps into a recipe. *Mise en place* is checking-in, giving the kitchen and your abilities a once-over to confirm you are able to complete the recipe. Do you understand all the terms that were used? Do you have the eight pans Julia Child believes you should in order to make the *gigot d'agneau pleureur*, or, for that matter, the patience? (I don't. I'm sorry.) It is simple but necessary work because it sets the tone for the rest of the process. Lingering over the details of the *mise en place* ensures less frantic and stressed action later in the baking.

The practice of *mise en place* is essential but often skipped. We assume a lot in this life, and we are no different in our kitchens. We plunge ahead because we've made *x* or *y* before so surely this is like all those times before. Often it is, until the dreadful moment it is not and we are affronted once more by the sickly quality of presumption. On our good days we promise ourselves to become the sorts of people who read the recipe through before starting it, and on our bad we blame the recipe for not coming with bolded warnings in advance cautioning us to not proceed until certain things had been accounted for.

Our spiritual lives are like that too. There is a *mise en place* of the self that should take place well before a new spiritual endeavor is begun, a check-in and evaluation, seeing if the ingredients and methods and equipment are all in place, ready for use. Though it has been often neglected in our conversations about Christian discipleship, the *mise en place* of the kitchen has a counterpart in the cadre of spiritual disciplines that is highly beneficial to us, called the Examen, and it is there we begin.

When giving the believers in Corinth instructions for Communion, Paul warned, "Let a person examine himself, then ... for anyone who eats and drinks without discerning the body eats and drinks judgment on himself.... But if we judged ourselves truly, we would not be judged."[17]

Paul cautions the believers to make careful inquiry about the state of their souls before receiving Communion, placing a great deal of emphasis on the honesty of their judgment, so that in judging rightly they do not invite the judgment of God on those things that they have overlooked, denied, or willfully ignored. If we fear our insufficiencies in this accurate reflecting, Paul has encouraged us in other places to depend on the power of the Holy Spirit within us, who "helps us in our weakness. For we do not know what to pray for as we ought, but the Spirit himself intercedes for us with groanings too deep for words."[18]

Over the centuries, Christians have approached this process of examination differently. Southern Baptists typically have a period of silent confession, of "making right with God" before receiving the Lord's Supper. Episcopalians confess their sins both aloud and silently before making peace with their fellow congregants and going to the Table together. Roman Catholics are strongly encouraged to go to confession before Mass. It varies by tradition, but Christian faithful of every kind tend to believe that some sort of diagnosis of the self is necessary before Communion is taken.

This may seem of little significance when many churches have made Communion a once-a-quarter ordinance, but for hundreds of years, beginning in the early church, Communion was a regular occurrence. Believers were in communities that observed the Lord's Supper at least weekly, if not daily. Such frequency made the examination of the self that Paul instructs us to undertake before receiving Communion a vital part of Christian living. Believers were told to call upon the Spirit to reveal to them the mysteries of their hearts. This intimate kind of prayer was eventually called the Examen, though you could say it was effectively the *mise en place* of the soul before spiritual work was undertaken. As receiving Communion became less frequent, the work of the Examen did not. It became a moving way to consider a believer's relationship with God each day.

One of the most popular and approachable methods of daily evaluation is the Ignatian Examen. Saint Ignatius, a priest and theologian in the fifteenth century and founder of the Jesuits, believed that God was active and present in the world and that careful and consistent engagement with God was the only way to devote oneself to Jesus in whatever was done during the day. There is something unique about Ignatius's presentation of the Examen, something wondrous: he tasks us to take into account more than our sins in need of confession. Ignatius asks us to consider and be mindful of the good works and loving responses we have shown to Jesus during the day. Ignatius believed that God cares as much about what we have done right as what we have done wrong. When in church we speak so often of our sinfulness and what we should do but never seem to manage to do, perhaps we could use a bit more reflection on what we do well. The Ignatian Examen is an invitation to hear as much about the love of God as the judgment of God.

We need to talk about your oven.

This is a component of the *mise en place*.

Ovens, no matter how modern, can heat unevenly and imperfectly. Many otherwise competent cooks have opened oven doors to discover dried-out chicken breasts and half-cooked frozen pizzas, all because one side of their oven heated differently than the other. This can be a particularly upsetting revelation when baking. Removing a half-charred, half-doughy mess as representative of one's first attempt at bread is not an auspicious start. Most ovens, though still uneven, are uneven with only a handful of degrees of difference. Your bread may still be a bit chewy on one end but it won't likely be a devastating discovery. There are cautions to be taken to avoid this possibility as best one can, though, and they are worth considering. This involves the investigation of hot spots, places in your oven where something would be heated more quickly than others.

Two methods I find the most satisfactory in discovering hot spots are using sliced bread or shredded coconut. With a rack placed in the middle, preheat your oven to 350F and arrange slices of bread or an even layer of shredded coconut on a baking sheet. Once preheated, slide the baking sheet onto the middle layer of the oven and leave to bake for a few minutes. Spend some time watching the bread or coconut through the oven window. Notice where it browns most quickly and least quickly. After five minutes, perhaps less if you're noticing things starting to char and burn, pull the baking sheet out. (If you used bread, you now have toast. If you used coconut, you now have toasted coconut for cookies.) This is a map of your oven. Where things browned most tells you where in your oven it gets the hottest; where things hardly browned at all, the coolest. In my oven, the back right corner is a culprit of excess heat, the middle left a bit too cool. Accordingly, when I bake or roast, I try and position my pan not too-close to that back right and a little off-center from the left so that things progress as evenly as possible.

Unfortunately, there's no solution to an oven that has dramatically disproportionate hot and cold spots all over, except to get a new oven. But most often, this is unnecessary, and simply knowing where in your oven things cook more or less quickly helps the process of making excellent food. Keep this knowledge in your working memory, and, as best as you can, always angle your pans where they will receive the most even heat coverage. If you have a particularly difficult hot spot, like a front left corner, you can always mitigate the damage by opening the oven door halfway through baking, rotating the pan, and then leaving it to finish baking evenly.

The Ignatian Examen is ultimately a practice of discernment. Or consider it like this: knowing the hotspots in your oven is like knowing the hotspots in yourself. The former you discover by practice and observation, the latter you discover by the same. Discernment is the ability to test the whims of this world, to judge rightly ourselves and our relation to God. For this reason, the writer of 1 John beseeches us: "Beloved, do not believe every spirit, but test the spirits to see whether they are from God, for many false prophets have gone out into the world."[19]

False prophets. A phrase that we shy from these days and, in some ways, rightly so. We are sometimes too trigger-happy with its employment, calling any sort of theology that we're not comfortable with a lie from hell. (And many of us have found ourselves on the receiving end of that accusation from fellow Christians.) But while discernment is a process that can help you evaluate the world around you, discernment must first begin in ourselves. What in us is a false prophet? What in us is leading us to false teaching? Along with the study of Scripture and the fellowship of other believers and our ongoing engagement with the Holy Spirit within us and made known to us in the Sacraments—the Examen refines in us our ability to divide what is our voice, God's voice, or something bad we ate for dinner that's back to haunt us in the middle of the night. Discernment is a lifelong process, for reflecting the likeness of Jesus that the image longs to show forth is also a lifelong process.

Ignatius championed his form of the Examen as the great equalizer of the faith, for the process of prayerfully considering ourselves is as necessary for priests as it is for farmers, for neither is beyond sinful action nor good deed. What we consider harmless today could strike us as sinful three years from now. What we consider sin today, in a handful of decades, only mistake. The Examen helps us be mindful of the whole of ourselves and, with that mindfulness, move about in the world with a bit more attention. Am I grumpy with my wife this morning because she said something that hurt my feelings, or is it really because I'm embarrassed that I forgot to take out the trash after she had asked several times? The Examen encourages our attentiveness, our care, for ourselves and for the world.

The practice of the Ignatian Examen is just that—practice. You're cultivating engagement with the Holy Spirit in a way that may be quite familiar or may be quite new. Practicing helps you learn the rhythms of discernment, the voice of God over the voice of yourself, and helps you identify your own impulses, both good and not so good. Ignatius followed a form that, adapted here for our use, can take longer if desired but could take as little as fifteen minutes before bed each day. Read this over, give it a *mise en place*, and then try it yourself this evening. This will be the spiritual practice for the week ahead at the close of each day.

1. Recognize that you are in the presence of God. Get still. Quiet your thoughts. Take a few deep breaths. Perhaps you should close your eyes or perhaps you should leave them open. Do what you need to do to feel alert but at ease. Be aware of the Holy Spirit within you, and pray that the Spirit would guide your questions, your evaluations, and your examination. Spend a few moments praying for clarity and charity toward yourself and others. Return to your stillness, recognizing God's presence.

2. Begin to think back on your day. At first, do not linger over anything. Simply consider the day as it is—who you met, where you went, what you felt, what you said. Consider how you spent your time, whether you ever felt flustered or peaceful. Let the day's rhythm become clear to you. Begin to thank God for the moments that were particularly enjoyable. It may take a moment to think of one or something may seem too small, but offer it back to God with thanksgiving all the same.

3. Now consider the day through careful discernment. During this day, what did you do that caused you to feel or to be far from God? What did you do that you wish you had not done? What did you

do that may have been sin? Take a moment to carefully evaluate what comes to mind. Ask the Holy Spirit if you have seen these things rightly. Have you assumed something was a sin that was only an accident? Have you ignored a sin and pretended it was only a mistake? As each comes to mind and each is evaluated, respond appropriately. To what was sinful, ask the forgiveness of God, and then release it to God. If there is peace to be made with your neighbor, rest in the knowledge that you will make it when you have the next opportunity. To what was only mistake, not sin, but may have been a source of shame or despair, thank the Spirit for helping you discern the difference and then ask for the healing that only the Spirit can bring. After each confession and each request for healing, imagine the thing being taken from you, released from you, and given back to God for God to worry about.

4. Now be mindful of what you did well. What moments made you feel close to Jesus? What moments most reflect to you the will of God being worked out in your life? Ask the Spirit if there was something ordinary in your day that has more significance than you first understood. Linger over the ways in which, small or large, you showed love to God, to God's world, to God's people. Thank God for God's partnership with you in this life, for the ways in which you come to know God more and more each day. Ask for God's continued guidance and to know God's love for you. Then, as before, allow these thoughts to loose from you. Give the good work back to God as well.

5. Ask the Holy Spirit to give you peace about the day and if there is anything in particular that the Spirit wants you to pay attention to from it. If something arises, dwell on it for a moment. Ask God what God desires you to see. Perhaps it is only to be mindful of it. Perhaps there is something you are to do. Pause over the thought until nothing new comes to mind, then give this too back to God. Ask the Spirit to return you to the place of peace.

6. Take a moment to think about the next day. Are there challenges ahead? Is it full of excitement? The unknown? Nothing out of the

ordinary? Thank God for bringing you through this day and seeing you into the next. Ask God for God's help in being attentive to yourself and the world around you as you go through tomorrow, thank God for God's help, and then offer this too back to God. End your prayer in a state of peace and, if you're inclined, an aloud, exhaled *amen*.

"The first one always fails."

We are in her kitchen in summer. I have just baked my first loaf of bread, and it is black on one edge and chewy in its center.

Constance is a professor of mine, but today she is the master baker in her own lived-in kitchen. I have driven the thirty miles from campus and reported at dawn, as instructed, and we have been at work pouring and shaping and waiting for six or so hours. The end result? A very quiet disaster of scorched grain on a slab.

Constance's kitchen is worth making note of. Its apparent features are usual enough: sink, refrigerator, wine rack, dishwasher. It's what hangs on the walls that sometimes throws people. Icons everywhere. Icons of Mama Mary holding forth the child Christ. Icons of Jesus the Good Shepherd. Icons of Saint Francis receiving the stigmata and Saint Mary Magdalene in the countryside of France—where, the tradition rumors, she ended her life after serving as a missionary to Europe professing the name of Jesus. I had asked Constance once about them.

"Icons serve as reminders of the working out of our salvation," she replied without looking up from the onion she was chopping. "They keep me always asking the question of what it means to be made in the image and likeness of God. What does that really look like?"

I said nothing in response because I wanted to seem as if I understood; it was years until I did.

Today, years since I asked that question, in front of the failed bread, I am indignant. Constance makes some of the best bread I have ever tasted, which is why I had first asked her to teach me how. I assume, immediately, that I do not have the gift for the work and it will remain forever beyond me. I am embarrassed, so I show it through anger. "So that's it, I just can't do it." I declare this from across the kitchen island that separates us, the charred and oozing lump between, Jesus the Good Shepherd watching from over Constance's left shoulder.

"Because of one loaf?" She laughs heartily. "Everyone fails with their first loaf. That's part of it. Now we do it again, but this time we go slow and we ask questions. We pay attention to where we were too hasty or too rushed or too inattentive. And then we'll do it again. And again. And again."

"It's a lot of work," I marvel.

She gestures a hand about the room, indicating our communion of saints, our watchers, our instructors. "Not unlike salvation. Not unlike figuring out the whole business of being in the likeness of Jesus." She smiles, then pushes the inedible mass aside, brings out a new bowl. "Now. Again."

Practicing the Ignatian Examen for the first time or practicing it for the fiftieth is a lot like that first charred loaf of bread I made in Constance's kitchen. Distraction, uncertainty, arrogance, misplaced criticism, frustration all come out in forces of varying degrees as you and the Holy Spirit try to make sense of your soul. At times, you'll find yourself wondering about that box left unchecked on your to-do list or whether you'll die alone. The mind, when given liberty to be still for a bit too long, has a tendency to bring up all kinds of shadowed doubts and terrors. Some days, these will be as easy to expel as flicking away a gnat. Other days, these will feel crippling.

Lean into the Holy Spirit. It is the Spirit, ultimately, who is the revealer and intercessor in this practice. Reach out to the Spirit for your help, your rootedness, your center. When you find thoughts straying, name them before God. "God, I'm distracted." And then wait, wait and see if your mind settles back. If it doesn't, take a moment to pay attention to what won't leave you alone. A friend has come to mind that you don't often think of. Their appearance in your mind's eye is persistent. Turn this over to God. Confess that you don't know why this person has been brought to mind. Take some time to pray for them. Pray blessing over them. Unless they have told you of a specific circumstance, do not pray beyond their well-being, their joy in the Lord, and God's favor to be upon them. Pray in this way until your prayers feel complete and you find yourself once again in a place of stillness. Offer this moment once more back to God and then begin right where you left off in the process of the Examen.

It's clumsy work, but we are clumsy beings. Knowing ourselves is a profound declaration of trust. Trust not only in our own ability to contend with our souls and bodies but also in God's willingness to reveal to us ourselves, caught up in the very life of God. Not just once, but over and over.

Now. Again.

As I said, it's true of practicing bread as well. This week, as you begin, set your goals reasonably. If you've never made bread before, go slow. Feel everything as it happens, get to know your bowls and your wooden spoons and the sponginess of dough beneath your palm. If you've done it too many times to count, look for the ways in which it can feel new again. Bread is a kind of miracle. If you take a moment to slow down, you'll glimpse it.

For This Week

DISCIPLINE

- This week, practice the form of the Ignatian Examen found on pages 44–46.

- Try to do the practice every day. You won't always be asked to try a spiritual discipline daily, but there is something deeply refreshing and emboldening about noting the rhythms of your soul from day to day.

- Pay attention to patterns, pay attention to what surprises you, but as the Ignatian Examen encourages, be careful in offering these observations back to God and not as evidence for self-criticism or occasions for arrogance.

BAKE

- Perform the *mise en place*—read through the recipe you will be using many times, consider any questions you may have.

- Map your oven for its hot and cool spots and learn the evenness with which it bakes or does not bake.

- Make some bread! This is the first go-round. Be generous with yourself and slather everything baked with as much butter as possible!

ASK

- Thinking about your experiences in church, have you found as much emphasis on the good things you do daily with Jesus as much as your sin? Why do you think this is?

- What do you find the most challenging instruction in the Examen to be? Why does it challenge you? Is it bringing out something new in you that you weren't aware of before?

- After reading this chapter, does the idea of discernment seem different to you? Does discernment play a role in your daily life?

Measure and Mix:
Lectio Divina

What cannot be taught by book or instruction but only by repetition is the very feel of dough, of when bread is properly risen, of the hollow sound it makes when it bakes just right. You won't become familiar with any of that unless you do it again and again. Constance's assurance that the first loaf always fails is a good one, but I also can assure you the first hundred and first thousand will also fail, comparatively. Each time you will learn something new. When you first make the loaf that tastes and feels good, you will think nothing can compare. Then you will make it again, and it will be just a bit better. What that has to do with measurement and mixing might not seem obvious, but feeling and quantity are irrevocably linked. Too much flour and the dough feels dry, too much water and the dough feels too sticky. An overwhelming thought, but be patient with both the process and yourself. For all its unforgiving ways, baking also happens to be one of the few things in life where the addition of a bit of flour or a bit of water can bring about salvation. That's a comfort of a kind. So much of the labor of good bread is simply the task of edging the dough away from the extremes of dry, crumbly brick and sodden, sticky mess.

Edging away from extremes has me thinking about Scripture.

Far too often we treat Scripture as a rulebook, announcing to us—and more than us, to everyone we disagree with—the unending *can'ts* and *don'ts* we think make up faithful lives. But what if we sought a better way? What if we saw Scripture as not to be memorized for the sake of apologetics, but for the sake of giving language to the beauty of this God-saturated world? Scripture gives us the measure of our belief, the mixture of our ways of perceiving how God moves in and through and around us.

For instance, the Psalms teach us we may wrestle with God and demand God's justice; the prophets teach us what faithless children we can be and yet God remains faithful to us; the creation accounts teach us about the God who forms worlds with extraordinary diversity; the Gospels that the same God comes into the midst of us; the epistles that we are not so different from the disciples two thousand years ago, fighting over the same things; and on and on and on, over and over.

Scripture is not a rulebook and it is not a catechism. Scripture is the multiplicity of genres and stories converging to tell the story of us and our relation to God and God's relation to us. But we often seek to master the Bible when it would have us simply sit with it, in its pondering and paradox and praise. For if we let it, like learning to feel the dough fully and intuitively, Scripture gifts us with the measure of ourselves, the mixture of different ways of being faithful.

Why does Scripture matter? Why should we pay so much attention to it?

In the gospel of Matthew, after Jesus is baptized he departs for the wilderness by the direction of the Spirit, where he fasts for forty days and forty nights. When he grows hungry, Satan comes to him: "If you are the Son of God, command that these stones become bread."[20] In reply, Jesus quotes a portion of Deuteronomy 8:3, "Man shall not live on bread alone, but on every word that proceeds out of the mouth of God."[21] When Jesus is tempted, his response is not to quote Scripture as proof text, but to quote Scripture as an exercise in active engagement with Scripture itself. Jesus does not only know the text in passing, but also speaks with authority and discernment. This is confirmed to us by what happens next:

> Then the devil took him into the holy city and had him stand on the pinnacle of the temple, and said to him, "If You are the Son of God, throw Yourself down; for it is written, 'He will command his angels concerning you'; and 'On their hands they will bear You up, so that You will not strike Your foot against a stone."[22]

Here, Satan has quoted Psalm 91:11 – 12. Satan knows the Scripture as well. Instead of Satan's previous temptation based on the physical, immediate needs of Jesus, the Accuser now suggests Scripture gives permission for the temptation. To this Jesus responds with Deuteronomy 6:16: "On the other hand, it is written, 'You shall not put the Lord your God to the test.'"[23] Jesus' knowledge of the Scripture is beyond rote. The Devil tries to twist the words, but Jesus puts the Scripture in conversation with itself. A portion of the Bible does not exist in isolation. Jesus rejects the trickery of Satan by knowing the whole, not just a part, of the Bible. His dismissal of the Tempter after the third temptation follows the same momentum.

Following this, in the gospel of Luke, we read:

And He came up to Nazareth, where He had been brought up; and as was His custom, He entered the synagogue on the Sabbath, and stood up to read. And the book of the prophet Isaiah was handed to Him. And He opened the book and found the place where it was written,

> *"The Spirit of the Lord is upon Me,*
>
> *Because He anointed Me to preach the gospel to the poor.*
>
> *He has sent Me to proclaim release to the captives,*
>
> *And recovery of sight to the blind.*
>
> *To set free those who are oppressed,*
>
> *To proclaim the favorable year of the Lord."*

And He closed the book, gave it back to the attendant and sat down; and the eyes of all the synagogue were fixed on Him. And He began to say to them, "Today this Scripture has been fulfilled in your hearing."[24]

Luke orders his gospel with a specific progression: Jesus shows his authority over the Scriptures against the Devil, then he shows that same authority against the leaders of this world. By the time he calls the first disciples, we have been introduced not only to Jesus as the one who heals the sick and raises the dead, but as the one who fulfills the Scriptures by completely understanding them, intimately and personally as well as for the community.

As modern Christians, we perhaps take this for granted; but, if we are reading or hearing these gospels as first- or second-century believers, we are being introduced to this Jesus. The emphasis is placed on revealing him as faithfully engaged with the Scripture that speaks of and points to him. Jesus has invited us, through the power of the Spirit, to know the Scripture as he does. Jesus shows familiarity and understanding in his approach. Whereas he could have rebuked Satan through his authority as God, Jesus rebukes Satan through his authority from Scripture. Whereas Jesus could have stood in the synagogue and declared himself the Messiah, he reveals this exceptional mystery through the authority of the Scripture. Jesus is offering to us the same kind of love of the Bible. The end of such biblical appreciation is not a set of arguments or the weight of proof, but openness to the Bible whereby we read it with the expectation that it is alive, inspired, vibrant, and is in the process of reading us as much as we are attempting to read it.

The Scripture opens us, changes us, causes us to inhabit the world differently, approaching the creation with a heart being molded into that of the Creator. We return to the image of that path; we return to the care of measurement, mixing. Scripture must read us more than we read it, we must come to know it like we know the balance of flour and water.

In an interview with Krista Tippett for *On Being*, Rabbi Lawrence Kushner, the renowned teacher of the Jewish mystical tradition, Kabbalah, told a story about a class of fourth graders visiting a synagogue where he was serving. The class was just about to see the Torah, which in synagogues is kept in the ark, behind the *parochet*, a curtain that signifies the holiness of what is behind it. Rabbi Kushner had not told the children what was behind the curtain except that it was very special. The class ran out of time, however, and the rabbi had to send them on their way with promises to open the curtain on their visit the next week. The following day, the teacher of the class reported to the rabbi what the students speculated was behind the curtain. The first suggested rather plainly that there was nothing behind it. The second, something holy to the Jewish people. The third, a car. The fourth, however, confident and sure, said that she believed that behind the curtain was a mirror.

An answer, the rabbi mused, concluding the story, that was not at all incorrect.[25]

Lectio divina is a discipline of reading Scripture that helps us be mindful of how the Bible is the mirror of our souls.

It's difficult to name any one person as responsible for conceiving the form of reading Scripture known as *lectio divina*, which means "divine reading." As early as the second century after Jesus, the term was being employed along with *lectio sacra*, "sacred reading," to refer to the intentioned hearing and internalizing of Scripture read aloud. The great early commenter on Scripture, Origen of Alexandria, believed that something mystical happened when the Bible was read by a believer, that Jesus was made known uniquely to us through meditation on the words inspired by the Holy Spirit. In a way, this was in keeping with the practice of the synagogues that for centuries had meditatively heard a reading from the Scriptures before inviting the opportunity to comment upon them. If the psalmist mused that God inhabited the praises of the people, the early Christian writers took the interpretation of such promise a step further and assigned the power of God's nearness and knowability to the reading of the Scripture itself.[26]

In the centuries following the rise of the early church in the West, as monastic communities started and flourished, the vocational calling of a life devoted to constant, perpetual prayer became one of the great goods of the church. Women and men vowed to serve Jesus through continual devotion in prayer, fasting, good works, tending the poor and sick. Men and women religious — monks and nuns as eventually they would be known — were the spiritual warriors of the church, standing on the frontlines of the ministry of the kingdom and calling all heavenly power to the aid of humankind. In the midst of this, Saint Benedict, the visionary of the Western monastic movement, saw Romans 10:8 – 10 as an invitation to engage the Bible as part of a vocational life of prayer.

But what does it say? "The word is near you, in your mouth and in your heart" (that is, the word of faith that we proclaim); because, if you confess with your mouth that Jesus is Lord and believe in your heart that God raised him from the dead, you will be saved. For with the heart one believes and is justified, and with the mouth one confesses and is saved.[27]

Benedict presented monasticism as built upon two principles: prayer and work. He emphasized the importance of Scripture not only learned but also dwelt in, teaching us how to pray, to think, to be in the world. Benedict's vision for approaching Scripture through a fourfold guided prayer was foundational in Western Christianity. Rather simply, Benedict suggested a small passage of the Bible be read slowly, repeatedly, and the Spirit invited to present something particular about the passage to the person. A simple habit of prayer, but a profoundly transformative one.

Hundreds of works in varying forms have been devoted over the years to employing his appreciation of the Scripture as an invitation to the personal work of the Holy Spirit in our lives. Even through the Reformation, *lectio divina* has been considered a faithful and trusted friend to the church that desires to encounter the Bible afresh again and again. John Calvin affirmed the good of the discipline and even the Puritan theologian Richard Baxter advocated the practice.

Into the twenty-first century, *lectio divina* remains one of the most revered and appreciated practices of Christians across denominational lines. Each proponent has maintained, in the line of Benedict and the line to Paul, that *lectio divina* is completely dependent on the guidance and inspiration of the Holy Spirit. Without the same Spirit who inspired the Scripture we read, we would be blind to them. *Lectio* is a surrendering to the movement and perspective of the Spirit in the Spirit's own words.

Getting messy is essential in bread making. While people are fond of bread machines these days, KitchenAid mixers with dough hooks—I am too, don't get me wrong—there's a lost art in sinking hands into a bowl of measured-out ingredients and getting to work.

This book is about prayer being bodied; so, as much as possible, body your bread making. Roll up your sleeves. Get messy.

(How appropriate to talk about messiness in a chapter about reading the Bible!)

If you're without a dough spatula—one of those plastic, flat devices that bend a bit when pressed—please get one. They are cheap but helpful. Just your hands will do, in a pinch, but the dough spatula boasts a versatility your fingers do not. When you're working with the loaf of bread on page 32, when you reach the section on initial incorporation of the wet and dry ingredients, this is when the delightful absurdity and overwhelming reality of gluten-laden chaos intersect. Go slow.

Begin by using your spatula to gently pull the flour into the water, gingerly guiding the two together. Give attention to the sides and bottom of the bowl so as to not end up with any dry lumps. Perhaps spin the bowl a bit with your hand, a little at a time. You're literally scraping here, gentle as the touch may be. Scrape along, fold, scrape, fold. The dough will begin to come together and form a loose, shaggy shape. This is when the mess truly takes over. Get your other hand in there, using the spatula to fold the dough on itself, and use your newly added hand to incorporate any leftover flour straggling around.

Cover the dough and let it alone for fifteen minutes. This process is called an *autolysis*, in which the water hydrates the flour. It will only be after this period that we have any real grasp as to whether or not the humidity of where we are requires the extra half cup or less of flour. The mess and the patience are well worth it, ultimately, because the best bread comes from it. Sort of like how the mess of us laid open by the Scripture is being patiently worked out as well, evaluated for what we might need a half cup more or less of in ourselves.

Madeleine L'Engle once wrote, "We think because we have words, not the other way around. The more words we have, the better able we are to think conceptually."[28] Think of it: the larger our vocabulary, the better to engage our reflections upon God. What we take from the Scripture we don't take in isolation, but in the community of those before and those surrounding us. A check on our hearts and intentions as we allow Scripture to form us is to put what we are discerning and learning in conversation with those faithful not just within our immediate circle, but with those in and across time. (We will discuss this more fully in the chapter "Forming: Rootedness.")

When the psalmists speak of the Scripture, they speak of it as unfolding. The Bible is not simply received, understood, and then put aside, but is always transformative. It is possible to think one way about a passage and return to it a year later with a renewed sense of perspective or meaning. We may be surprised what is significant to us later in life that was not before, or we now consider as unfaithful that which was not so in our youth.

The first disciples prove this. Before receiving the Holy Spirit, the disciples walk with and learn from Jesus for three years. They slowly—sometimes painfully slowly—learn the way of grace that he is revealing to them, begin to glimpse the meaning of the kingdom of God, the strangeness of its abundance. But even after three years, it is not until the Holy Spirit is given that the secret of the Scripture is slowly revealed to them. Jesus promised before his ascension in Acts, "You will receive power when the Holy Spirit has come upon you."[29] We accept this passage often as given: the disciples were able to heal the sick, raise the dead, follow in the way of Jesus. However, we do not often recognize this power of the Spirit as being able to discern and interpret the Bible, though one of the first manifestations of the Holy Spirit upon the disciples at Pentecost is the preaching of Peter to the assembly outside. In that sermon, Peter quotes numerous passages of the Old Testament and prophetically interprets and explains their meaning as speaking to the coming of the Messiah and the fulfillment in Jesus.

Skeptics of *lectio divina* worry that in our highly individualized culture, people will assume that everything they feel or sense or conclude will lead them to believe they are infallible. This is remedied by a simple caution and reminder: we do theology in community, not isolation. The Holy Spirit may lead us as individuals in particular ways, encountering a passage of Scripture uniquely to the context we find ourselves in. But we should be wary of making doctrine out of that experience. We bring our interpretations to the faithful community, past and present. We learn to discern together, not only individually. *Lectio divina* is not a replacement for Bible study, sermons, commentaries, historical criticism. *Lectio divina* is about opening ourselves to the work of the Spirit through the power of the inspired Scripture. The Scripture offers us immediate engagement with God and immediate engagement with one another, an invitation to continual transformation, refinement, and shaping. The careful mixing of our souls.

I poured a pan of hot caramel onto a sheet of buttered parchment once on the oval table in this Scottish kitchen, and it left a permanent darkness on the Formica surface where the heat pulsated through. The mark is like a bruise, smeared purple-brown. I vow to you when I put my hand over it all these months later I can still feel the heat. Maybe that's how things are in this world—the heat gets in something, the chill gets in, it lingers. The shape of the bruise on the table is like the smear of blood over the doors of the faithful in the Passover, an arch splintering at both ends. God warns any who do not make the sacrificial meal and do not smear the blood of the lamb over their doorposts that they will have their firstborn taken from them into death.

"It's the threat of ending their story." Tom is leaning in the doorway of the kitchen while I am turning a loaf over atop the bruise of the table. We are discussing Exodus. He's a theologian, in the technical sense, and when he speaks of the Bible I listen differently. He loves it, but he also distrusts himself in relation to it; so he's never quick to be certain about his own convictions, a habit I marvel at in him and do not find readily in myself. "If the firstborn is killed," he explains, "then the story of that family, the memory of that family, the inheritance and all that comes with it, is essentially cut off. Who will there be to remember? Who will there be to carry on? There may be siblings, maybe, but they are considered culturally second best. God's last plague is a threat to end the history of Egypt itself because there won't be a generation to tell their stories for them."

I bring the butter from the counter, pick up the bread knife. It runs through the loaf easily. I cannot think of anything but death in this moment; the knife goes quickly, the bread splits free. The Israelites are told to eat their meal quickly, with intention but quickly, because Egypt will want them gone immediately after death visits them.

"So if it's not about being set free from the pharaoh, or perhaps not only about that, what's it about?" I hand him a bit of bread.

He shrugs. "Exodus is a book about telling the story." He takes the slice, dips a knife on the table into the butter. "God doesn't spend a lot of time saying God is doing these things to get people out of Egypt. That shows up a few times but not many. Most of the time, God says God is doing these things so Israel will be able to tell the story to their children. To tell their children. And theirs. It's why in the seder meal the command is to tell the story of the Exodus. You don't read it out of the Torah word for word and then say you're done. You tell the story. You embellish. You forget and someone else reminds you. You tell it again."

He takes a bite of the bread and I consider this. I cross to the double doors overlooking the wood and note my breath still shows against the glass, even in the early days of spring. The chill gets in. The heat gets in. The stories get in our bones. "So telling the stories, in a way, is more important than the stories themselves." I look back at him and he is nodding slowly.

"I wouldn't say that without saying a lot of other things. Scripture is inspired, important; it's more than just a story. But if you're looking for the reason we read it so much in the first place, the reason that God tells Israel to keep telling the stories over and over, that has to do with how those stories tell us a lot about who God is and how God wants to be known to us and how the world works and how the world should be. That's the work of the Spirit, helping us grasp it."

We return to the path.

A friend of mine, an Episcopal priest, reminded me, Jesus often tells his disciples not to announce to everyone what they have just heard or seen. For as many times as they are sent out, they are also told to stay and ponder. *Lectio* is a discipline that invites stillness, to get our hands messy. We read Scripture to be read by it in turn, to hear from it what the Spirit would tell us. Cultivating in ourselves the confidence to hold on to the message intended only for us is the difficult task. When we don't immediately externalize what we have understood, we are forced to deal with it in ourselves. We are forced to see understanding as a process, not a single event. This too is an act of measuring, the measuring of ourselves. We have to keep our hands in the bowl. We have to keep the dough worked until it's done. It's another way of getting at the path we're on. We are learning the feel and look of the path beyond not just by the weight of our feet against the dirt, but what sort of dirt it is in the first place, what sort of world this is after all, beyond the limits of what we can grasp.

There are different ways of reading through the Bible, and all of them can be used with *lectio divina*. From my earliest days I can remember the printed sheets in my parents' church, fresh every January 1, a rhythm of Psalms, Old Testament, New Testament, that would culminate in reading the Bible through in its entirety by the end of the year. Then it was to be begun again. There are chronological reading plans — perhaps better described as narrative-focused reading plans — and reading plans that have you read the Bible in full four or five times before the year is out. I see advantages to all approaches. In the end, you are engaging with the Scriptures.

Personally, I prefer the daily lectionary ordered in the 1979 Book of Common Prayer, but it's not the only one. Lectionaries are cycles of readings that bring together a psalm, Old Testament, New Testament, and gospel reading each day, usually in a two-year cycle. They are not unique to Christianity, however, and date as far back to, according to the Talmud, the time of Moses, when certain portions of Torah were assigned on appointed days of feasting and fasting. Lectionaries put Scripture in conversation with itself, focusing our attention on how the church has seen the Scriptures working through the years and how God might be speaking to us in the pauses between the readings, when gospel and Old Testament are put across from one another. I tend to choose a reading out of the lectionary cycle for my own *lectio*, but you should feel free to use any cycle of Bible readings most comfortable to you.

Depending on the amount of time you have, you will want to limit how many verses of Scripture you focus on. I've found that a passage of about ten verses takes me about fifteen to twenty minutes.

1. When you've chosen your passage, take a moment to get still. Remind yourself you are in the presence of God and God is present to you. Breathe slowly. Be patient. Ask the Holy Spirit to guide your reading.

2. Read. *Lectio* is quiet work. Read the passage you have chosen slowly, tenderly. Savor the words of the text. At the same time, notice if a particular word or phrase stands out to you. It will likely not come with any great thundering announcement, but rather a note of interest, intrigue, a sense of attention for the day. If nothing quite presents itself, be open to reading the passage again. Sometimes even a bit of familiarity allows for more focus during the reading.

3. Meditate. Consider the word or the phrase. Repeat it a few times in the silence of your heart. Feel it out. See what memories or ideas or anxieties or joys come to mind. There is no distraction in *lectio*. Scripture has a comment on everything about us, so give the Holy Spirit the freedom to let the Scripture pierce you and mend you. Take a few minutes to notice how the word or phrase makes space in you, what it draws out, what it directs you toward. Reread the passage. See how the word or phrase that has stood out to you works within the text itself.

4. Pray. Offer these meditations back to God. Ask for God's continued guidance and direction; thank God for the gift of the Scripture and the insight it stirs in you. Reread the passage, but this time as an act of surrender, marveling, wonder.

5. Contemplate. Return to the original posture of stillness. You may find yourself continuing to dialogue with God about what

you have understood, or perhaps you find yourself blessing and thanking God for the Scripture. Continue in the rhythm of sharing and stillness until you find yourself in silence. Reread the passage of Scripture, offering it back to God and as invitation to be near you throughout the day. Close with a simple *amen*.

For This Week

DISCIPLINE

- This week, practice *lectio divina* using the form found on pages 62–63.

- Practice the discipline at least three times this week. Daily is great if you can manage it, but commit yourself to three intentioned moments of encountering the Holy Spirit in the Scripture.

- Notice how *lectio* shapes you. Notice how the Scripture becomes closely knit to your thoughts. Pay attention throughout your day to ways in which the Scripture is more readily apparent to you than it has been before.

BAKE

- Focus on the texture of this week's loaf. Notice when it is too wet or too dry. Put your hands on it often, internalizing the information it gives you about itself.

- Consider trying one of the alternate ways of baking the bread described in the recipe instructions. How does this method change the quality of the bread? Do you like one version over the other?

- Compare this week's loaf to last week's. What's different or what's the same? What do you notice about the texture, the crust, the sponginess of the inside? Consider what improved, what didn't.

ASK

- How has your view of Scripture changed over time? What was it like when you were a child, a teen, a young adult, and so on? Perhaps you came to faith late in life and Scripture was something other people read and you have now read only recently. How has that shaped your approach?

- The limit of *lectio* is in the deeply personal nature of it. We discussed briefly the way theology is shaped in community. Can you think of a time when you presented what was more personal conviction than word for a community as if it were for a community? How did that go? What did you learn?

- When we come to Scripture, we bring our whole selves to it for examination and refinement. How has this past week shaped how you see yourself in relation to Scripture? How has Scripture commented on your week?

Kneading: Intercessory Prayer

～≫≫≫— ≪≪≪～

As previously mentioned, some people love their bread makers and forego the work of kneading altogether, while others have come to invest in sturdy stand-mixers well equipped for the job. I am in the latter camp, but I return often to the physical work of kneading bread myself because I find it grounding. It reminds me I have a body, a body gifted with the ability to labor. (Not everyone is, which makes stand-mixers miracles.) Years ago, under Constance's watch in her kitchen of patient saints, we returned often to the subject of kneading. Kneading is the life-making work of bread baking, dough beneath hands stretched and rolled and righted and upended. Kneading is what activates the gluten in flour, stretching it out just to the point of breaking so that when the dough bakes, these stretched pockets fill out full, big, giving bread lightness and robustness at the same time. Another reason we're focused on one loaf of bread over the course of this book is that kneading, like mixing, is a work requiring patience and intuited practice. Kneading is about the feel and the knowing that only comes between yourself and a loaf grown familiar to you through the years.

Intercession, like kneading, is a work that is both essential and often neglected. Often we imagine intercession is the focus of the spiritually significant, those great champions of belief. I often think of myself as incapable of any sort of disciplined focus of prayer. Some people are gifted with the clarity of particularity, able to spend hours wrestling with God on one particular matter or event. Not all of us are so gifted, and while such focus can be habituated in part, the gift itself cannot be taught. But this is not all there is when it comes to the work of intercessory prayer. So this week, we're getting our physical and spiritual hands working.

Too often, prayer is either presented as a wish-making transaction in which an amount of piety is traded for the price of a miracle or as this odd, passive work on the part of God that has nothing to do with God and everything to do with us bending ourselves to accept God's will, which has already been decided. Prayers for the sister to live or the meeting to go well only "work" if a certain number of years of church attendance are promised. Or the prayers are ultimately pointless because the outcome is unchangeable; it's just we who need to get on board with God's unwavering and meticulous plan.

But intercessory prayer, like all prayer, is conversation with God. It's conversation with someone so intimate and near to us, we can risk the deepest parts of ourselves in the exchange. We've been spending a few weeks now acquainting ourselves with the work of the Spirit in showing us who we are and who God is. This week we move into a posture of bringing those things together. I don't know how you were taught to pray, if you were taught at all. But intercessory prayer can be a casual or a formal thing. It can be silent or it can be out loud. But intercessory prayer is not to barter God into doing what we want, and it's not to wear us down into wanting what God has already decided; it's something much more beautiful. Intercessory prayer is how we talk with God and ask for help for ourselves and on behalf of others. (Some may balk—intercession, by definition, cannot be for yourself. I'll elaborate on this shortly.)

Through Jesus we have been adopted into the life of God and made temples of the Holy Spirit. The power of the Spirit in us enables us to reach out to the Father in the same way Jesus does. This is why Paul writes, "For through [Jesus] we both have access in one Spirit to the Father."[30] Jesus tells the disciples to pray to God as *Father*— intimate, personal—in the Lord's Prayer. The word *Father* there is not about a gendered distinction, but the assurance of our adoption into the family of God. Just as Jesus knows God in this way, so now we know God in this way. If we are truly in the family of God, "heirs of God and co-heirs with Jesus," as Paul also says, we are able to ask of God with the same boldness and conviction of Jesus.

Consider this brief episode in the gospel of Luke:

> Then Jesus told them a parable about their need to pray always and not to lose heart. He said, "In a certain city there was a judge who neither feared God nor had respect for people. In that city there was a widow who kept coming to him and saying, 'Grant me justice against my opponent.' For a while he refused; but later he said to himself, 'Though I have no fear of God and no respect for anyone, yet because this widow keeps bothering me, I will grant her justice, so that she may not wear me out by continually coming.'" And the Lord said, "Listen to what the unjust judge says. And will not God grant justice to his chosen ones who cry to him day and night? Will he delay long in helping them? I tell you, he will quickly grant justice to them. And yet, when the Son of Man comes, will he find faith on earth?"[31]

Jesus uses hyperbole to make his point. Of course God is infinitely better than the unjust judge, but he tells this story to remind the disciples it is the persistence of the woman who seeks justice that is commendable. She does not seek something flippant. She seeks justice, something the Old Testament frequently reminds us is dear to the heart of God. Of course, justice is not the only thing dear to God. The woman could have also been seeking safety, mercy, liberation, flourishing, and a number of other aspects of God's revealed character. It is implied the woman not only has a right to demand justice of the judge because of his position but also because justice is fundamental to the good of the world. Her persistence reflects this knowledge, and the judge's eventual relenting—either out of annoyance or conviction we might debate—indicates he is aware of this tension himself. He relents, perhaps, out of a suspicion that sooner or later justice will come.

When Jesus compares God to the judge, his point is not only God is better than the judge, but also God will readily bring about justice because it is fundamental to God's identity. God is not passive, waiting for us to accept the big and mysterious plan. God is ready to spring up and into action, here in the present moment. But then, of course, we arrive at the problem of the genie granting miracles. If God is so ready to arise and bring about justice, why are so many causes in this world in need of that justice seemingly unanswered? Why when we cry out to God for aid does it not come?

I don't know that anyone has a satisfying direct answer for this. There are a handful of things to be said that get at the answer just beyond our reach, in the void between this life and the life to come. When we make intercession, when we reach out to God and ask for God's help, a lot is contained within that. We could be like the widow in the parable, asking for help in the form of justice. Or perhaps we are asking for a sister to live, for help with the threat of death. Or perhaps something doesn't make any sense at all, seems like chaos from chaos, and the help we ask for is clarity, a way of seeing through. I think all intercession, ultimately, boils down to asking God for help. It's why I find the usual formula of asking God for something and God responding with *yes* or *no* or *wait* to be too narrow. I don't think God ever says *no* when we ask for help, but perhaps God says *not this way* or *not like this*. The rainy day when there should have been sun. Is this unanswered prayer? Trite as it may seem, that's often how we think of it. But let's press it further—the sister dies. The sister dies and the usual comfort is supposed to be God has a plan we can't see. The usual comfort is that our prayer was answered, it's just not the answer we want. That's fine when it rains on the day there was to be sun, when the path we are taking is mired in mud and muck and wet, but it's no great comfort in the mudslide, in the derailing, in the cataclysm when there was supposed to be smooth ways ahead.

Barbara is unpacking boxes in the community kitchen where her office for spiritual direction has temporarily relocated while the church education building is renovated. The priest is coming over later in the evening to ask blessing over the new space. In her old office, she had gone down to the river and taken stones to be placed inside some of its walls. This is an old tradition, medieval French, something about the image of water and its continual work on the rocks, smoothing them out into something kinder than what they once were. The tradition is supposed to signify that the work of the home—or in this instance, the office for spiritual direction—is one of softening, smoothing, peacemaking.

I've heard Barbara say this is like the Spirit of God in and upon us, the great Water rushing gentle and slow and fast and turbulent in tune with the seasons, again and again making our rough edges smooth.

I ask her about unanswered prayer, the season in which I dwell in God's silence. In this new space, she's without the stones. The walls are already built and sealed. Her hand presses to one with gentle recognition, then she turns back to me: "Preston, do you know who my favorite person in the Old Testament is?"

"No," I reply.

"Hannah. Not because she was barren and God opened her womb, but because she went again and again to the place of God and demanded God pay attention to her. Even the priest didn't understand how she was so confident that God listened to her. He thought she must be drunk. I don't love Hannah because eventually God gave her a son." Barbara smiles, deep and full. "I love Hannah because she's proof that God can take our anger, God can take our frustration. God wants it, I think. God wants conversation that's not all supplication and fear and bowing low. God wants anger. God wants the mess. God wants all the rough edges of us over and over and over so that the Spirit can rush over them again and again and soothe and smooth and comfort." She pulls the coffee pot from the counter, finds two cups. She sets these in front of me—my work—and turns back to the boxes she was unpacking—hers.

Barbara pulls up from one box an icon of Jesus with a shepherd's staff, lamb about his neck, called the icon of the Good Shepherd.

"He's not about answers the way we like to think of them." She touches the face of Jesus, seeming to have gone elsewhere from this world. "He's about seeing it better than we do. About grieving with us the death, the destruction, the decay. Because God does not will anyone to suffer, but we suffer. God does not will anyone be destroyed, but we destroy." She turns back to me. She is old and it shows these days more than most. "The Incarnation is the Good Shepherd coming to us and saying, 'I too hate this. I too wish for better. I too want it to be well.' But that's the thing. He is making *everything* beautiful in its time, and we want now, only now, right now.[32] We'll miss a better story if we insist on knowing the ending too soon."

"That's not exactly comforting."

Barbara shrugs. "I think that depends on where you believe comfort comes from: the answer to prayer in the way you wanted it to look or in the certainty that Jesus is in the midst of you while the great sadness occurs. I've lived many versions of a life." She moves to the stoneless wall, positions the icon upon it. "I take most comfort in the answerless Shepherd who at least keeps close."

Why do we knead?

Kneading activates the amino acids in flour, which give dough its shape and elasticity. In dry flour, these amino acids are curled up, unactivated, which is why you can shake off a bit of flour or pile it up or toss it in the air and not have it come back a ball. The amino acids are activated when the flour is bound together—with water, sugar, salt, and yeast—and they are stretched and pulled and given the space to extend their anthropomorphic limbs and give shape and structure. The autolysis is when the amino acids slowly unfold, giving the dough some lift, early signs of structure. Kneading stretches and expands the gluten, allowing it greater area to rise when it rests again. Kneading is an essential process not because without it we have no bread, but because without it our bread does not have good texture, form, or stability.

Likewise, intercession may not be necessary for the work of the Spirit in us, but a great deal of what gives us shape and form and stability depends on it.

How do we intercede?

We've talked around this, which is because it looks differently for a lot of people. Here's what it looks like for me. I go into my kitchen and knead dough. I get my hands right into the mess. (Or, when bread is not to be made, I usually lift my hands, palms up.) I talk to God. I tell God everything I have in mind about the situation, not unlike the opening of this book when we prayed blessing over our kitchens. When it's all out—the joy, the worry, the wonder—I get still. I listen. Maybe I feel a prompting, a leaning, the edge of something. Maybe I feel the Spirit tugging me toward some action or perhaps toward a different topic. I wait. Then I begin again. I open my mouth and let it all out. I empty. I bring the earnest everything of self before God. Then I see what happens. Sometimes that's five minutes. Sometimes it's five years. Depends on the topic. But close friends are like that.

And for this reason I believe intercession for ourselves is possible, because we are all connected. No one situation is so removed from everyone and everything else that we are not somehow connected to it. When we intercede, we are asking God to work good in the midst of something. Sometimes that means we will find ourselves in the position to give justice when we thought ourselves the ones owed it. Sometimes we discover the bad weather is misery to us but blessing to someone else. When we intercede, when we trust God enough to offer everything back in prayer, however brief or however long, we discover how every circumstance exists in relation to everyone else. It opens us to pray wholly. It emboldens us to see more of how God sees, the whole of the world, not just us, not just our requests, the Good Shepherd of all the sheep as well as of the one.

Kneading, like intercession, is about endurance.

After you have added the yeast mixture and salt to the dough and slowly worked it in, it's time to begin the longest work.

On a clean workspace, sprinkle a bit of flour onto the surface. (Take this flour from the ½ cup you reserved, per the recipe from page 32.) A good deal of flour is not needed; you only need enough flour to keep the dough from sticking. Turn your dough out onto the floured surface and give your hands a gentle, small dusting of flour. Shape your dough into an oval, doing your best to use the heels of your hands to shape. Fingers in dough cause it to lose texture and form. As much as possible, keep your fingers immobile, treating your hands like flat baker's paddles.

Once an oval, fold the dough halfway toward yourself, then after a very gentle dusting of flour from the ½ cup—a tablespoon, if that—press the folded dough down, gently, and roll it away from you. Turn the dough a quarter-turn, fold it halfway toward you, and gently roll it away with your heels once again. Don't bear down on the dough, pressing every last bit of air out of it. Don't press so deep that the sticky inside of the dough becomes exposed. If it does, do your best to turn the dough, fold, and very gently roll it back to stasis with the heels of your hands. As you work, if you notice the dough turning sticky to the point of being uncooperative, sprinkle a bit of the remaining flour on top of the dough to incorporate as you knead. Always knead a few times between additions of flour before adding more to be certain more is required. If it's your fingers that turn sticky with dough and they become unusable in the process, coat your hands with flour and then rub them together to clean them off before returning to kneading. Don't use water to rinse them as you'll introduce more water to the dough.

Just under seven minutes of kneading or slightly over—sometimes as soon as five, as long as ten—check the dough. You should have a soft, stretchy, springy form. If you gather it gently together into the shape of a ball, you should be able to press against the surface gently and then watch it spring back into shape. This is a sign of good gluten development, what makes the bread light and full. After this point, the dough is ready to rest and you are ready to wash your tired hands.

As a general guide, you'll know if your dough is under-kneaded if it is a shaggy mess and doesn't hold its shape. This is an indication that the dough needs more time. You will reach a point where you feel the dough give way to a silken texture and this is the first sign that the dough has been well kneaded. Conversely, an overkneaded loaf is sort of at a loss. On the one hand, it's extremely unlikely to happen when you knead by hand because of how you'll likely have tired yourself out long before the dough is overkneaded, but if I have learned anything in the kitchen it is that such possibilities do turn into realities more often than not. If the dough does not fold well, does not give easily when trying to knead it, then it's time to throw up your hands. When it rises, let it go a bit longer to see if during the rise a miracle might happen. If not, you'll end up with an extremely dense loaf of bread that, while not suited to sandwiches or slathering with butter, may after a day or two of being left out to dry and crust become an excellent basis for bread pudding.

Kneading is a work of wrestling, of working out something from chaos into something that has form. Intercessory prayer is like that. We are working out with God the mess of things, the chaos of being, and seeing what shape and form it could take on when we turn it over, again and again, back to God.

In the Old Testament and, we can safely assume of the Jews in the New, you pray with your body. There's not a lot of bow-your-head-and-close-your-eyes in the Old Testament. There's dancing and standing and lifting hands and making a lot of noise. Lament is loud and languid, cries that go on into the night. Joy is tambourine and frenzy.

Somewhere along the way, I imagine around the time we became phobic of the physical body altogether and praised fasting more than feasting and abstinence more than marital sex, we stopped seeing prayer as bodied. We reduced praying to bowed heads and closed eyes and silence. It's hard to think, though, that being caught up in the life of God has to be as quiet as only bowed heads and only closed eyes. Only ever that.

God speaks forth creation and when God comes to us as a baby crying in the cold springtime night in the Incarnation or as rushing wind on Pentecost with tongues ablaze, it's hard to think of God as the quiet type, at least exclusively.

When I knead, I pray. Kneading is kinetic, connected with the work of shaping and guiding dough. It's perhaps a bit too easy to see the connection: intercession is a work that is shaping and guiding me. When I knead, prayer seems obvious, because prayer is patient work but it does not have to be quiet work, as with kneading. When I feel rage, deep rage, the old rage of injustice, I put a loaf on the board and work out the loud words of the psalmists, demanding the God of justice show up as the God of justice has promised to do. When death sits in the corner counting someone's hours down, another loaf is turned out and these hands of mine learn the slower work of miracle asking or peace seeking.

In every season, a different prayer, a different bread, a different way of bodying the connection to the God who hears all, sees all, fills all. The connection we all share, together.

Constance told me once baking bread is by nature a relational work because even the slightest changes become felt, become known. I think of intercession like that. It's a way of coming to know myself as I think God knows me — what I really care about underneath it all, what's lurking there needing answer. The dough becomes a kind of mirror in the same manner as the Scripture: I bring heaviness to the kitchen counter, I walk away lightened.

What's the line of the old hymn? "I'll drop my burden at His feet and bear a song away."[33]

Maybe dough isn't your intercession work. Maybe it's the drive to drop the kids off or the fifteen minutes before rising out of bed. But this week, give yourself permission to let prayer be free. Lift hands or bend knees. Shout loud or sing soft. Pour out yourself, your prayer, and then get still. Get still and wait and hear. Maybe there will be nothing; maybe there will be thunderclaps. Maybe. Intercession is the hardest discipline to describe because the rewards seem tangled: what is the proof that it has worked? The justice comes, the sick rise again? The stone of self is smoothed? Maybe. Maybe the answer, as the poet said, is there is "no bridge but the thread of patience."[34]

Unlike our previous weeks, the practice of intercessory prayer is less formulaic. Let this week be one of tender focus. Next week, we enter a time of stillness, so let these days here mark a dedicated loudness in you, however that is made known. Let intercessory prayer be a thing in your hands, in your feet, in whatever posture feels the most honest. Get your body in the thick of prayerful labor. Let prayer get in your bones, in your limbs, the way dough and its feel indents itself against fingers and bowls and teaches you its secrets by its touch.

As general guidance, I have suggested some specific things to focus your prayers on for the week. Take ten to fifteen minutes each day, perhaps longer, to prayerfully consider the day's theme. Whether you're driving around and making time during traffic, standing at your kitchen island working your dough, or taking a moment in the quiet of the morning, turn your focused thoughts to the power and nearness of Jesus and sit with him for a little while, tell him what's on your mind.

Suggested Points of Focus

- *Monday:* Pray for family near and far. Pray for the lost, the ones who feel far from Jesus. Ask the Good Shepherd to continue to seek them out and to use you in whatever way he would to be a reminder of his deep love and grace for them. Pray for your parents, your children, your spouse. Pray for their deepening knowledge of God, for their awareness of God's love for them.

- *Tuesday:* Pray for your work. Whatever your work is, offer it back to God. Pray for those you come into contact with, for those in authority over you and those you have authority over. Pray that in all ways you may be a representative of the love of Jesus and that you would be open to the ways in which Jesus may surprise you by their example and goodness toward you.

- *Wednesday:* Pray for your country. Pray for the leaders and directors of local and national policy. Pray that in all they do the justice and mercy of God would be made known by and through them, that they would defend the marginalized and oppressed and keep foremost in their concern the cause of the needy. Pray that in word and deed they would execute their office with the patient kindness of the Servant-King Jesus.

- *Thursday:* Pray for your church and its ministers. Pray that by their lives and doctrine they would do all good works God has fashioned them for and to lead God's people. Pray for the protection of their hearts against pride, against fear, against insecurity. Pray for a sense of God's delight and favor to be made known to them.

- *Friday:* Pray for those who are in suffering. On the day our own Lord suffered the cross, pray for those who suffer in this life. Pray for wisdom for those who care for them, for the overturning of powers and authorities that keep them oppressed, for the swift justice of God to rescue the afflicted.

- *Saturday:* Pray for the dead. Pray that those who have died in horror shall not have died in vain. Pray for the restoration of God's justice and might in the world. Pray against the powers of the devil and the works of evil that terrorize the world. Pray against all hatred and malice, all contempt and dehumanization, for the earth in need of healing and for the children of God in need of protection.

- *Sunday:* Pray for new life. Pray for the Church around the world, that as they begin or end or find themselves in the midst of worship services today and throughout the week that the love of Jesus would reverberate through all they do and proclaim. Pray that God's favor and generous wonder would be imparted to all who seek God this day, wherever and however they seek God.

For This Week

DISCIPLINE

- This week, practice intercession. (Simple, right?) Use the suggested focuses found on pages 75–76.

- Notice yourself in prayer—what is your typical posture, what do you feel yourself leaning toward and into? Don't try to make sense of any of that, don't force your own hand. Observe.

- Work through the themes, but don't feel bound to them. Let your prayer move as you move, an amalgamation of Spirit and self. See what comes to mind, what is taken from you. Intercession is a work, but it is also a release. Leave the work at the metaphorical altar, wherever you find and make it.

BAKE

- Practice light and gentle hands. Feel every last bit of the bread beneath your hands. Feel it give and pull.

- Notice how the bread sticks some then becomes smooth. Notice how your hands come to know the movement when the dough turns silk, just on the rim of completion.

- As before, take stock of the loaf this week in comparison to last. How is kneading changing for you? Are your hands lightening? Are you unburdening yourself?

ASK

- Do you believe you're allowed to get angry with God? Not just angry, but to wrestle with God, confront God, expect of God?

- The tension of prayers that feel unanswered can root deep in us. Are there unanswered prayers lingering in you? Does this feel like the work of the stone smoothing or have you held that back from the water of the Spirit?

- Intercession assumes closeness with God, even when unfelt. Ponder that. What does that mean for your own life?

In the World

Over the next three weeks, we consider disciplines focused on cultivating our relationship to God in the creation. We will first explore how the goodness of the world is made known to us, then how the Christian tradition teaches us humility, and finally, how we may discover places of remembrance in the world that keep us focused on God.

Here is where we continue, wanderers on this path. We look from ourselves to the world around us, where God is to be found in surprise, where God is to be found at great work.

Rising: Wonder

When I was living at the end of the world, on the edge of the sea in Scotland, I was inducted into the hard work of wonder. Along the path cutting through the wood from my apartment into town, the earnestness of a busy life melted. The path was typically unpeopled, except a few here and there. Wandering into solitude by circumstance, not by design, it became of great importance to reconcile myself to the situation. By nature I am not solitary, at least not for extended periods of time. Isolation is appealing only in bursts, in moments of late evening or early morning, ushering out of or into the day. But none of my friends lived on my end of the path, though they would walk it to come to dinner or coffee, and in turn I would walk it back with them. That often left me alone. Eventually, when there were no new podcast episodes to be played or no money to put toward yet another audiobook, I found I was alone completely. It was only me and myself. Even that left me too, when the chattering of my own mind became so boring I couldn't endure it any longer. I found myself, one day in December, the day of the first snow that would not melt until spring, alone on the path. I had become still.

Stillness might be easier described by what it is not than what it is. Stillness is not exclusively silence, though it can be like that. Stillness is not meditation, though it can be like that too. Stillness is what Ellen Langer, a professor of psychology at Harvard University, describes as attention, as a habituated sense of new discovery. She describes how, if you ask yourself to see something new in someone you have known a long time, it might surprise you what you find. The person becomes mysterious in a way, exciting and unexpected. Langer goes on to insist such work is not a thing one enters into and steps out of, practicing the awareness as a way to cope with the rest of a busy day. Rather, awareness is a constant, something we inhabit in everything we do. From her point I go some steps further: awareness is what leads us into wonder. Enchantment. Praise.

On the December day I found myself alone, I slowed my pace, studied the skyline, and eventually stopped beneath a crooked tree with a single crimson leaf still clinging to a barren branch. There was a bit of wind that lifted it, up and up, urging release, but the leaf would not let go. It was then, by such simple observation, the wonder of trees, of their seasons, their age, their circling forms of seed to flowering to earth and over again, became present to me as if for the first time. What changed in me? What had chanced the sudden awe? Experience tells me it was nothing more than the step taken just beyond quieting myself.

As we have already discussed, bread making requires a good deal of patience and trust. There is only so much we can do to bring the ingredients together. At a certain point we have to forfeit control and trust for the best. We must trust the dough will rise. We must trust the slow work is rewarding work. I am reminded of Simone Weil's words about the work of God in our lives: "The action of grace in the heart is secret and silent."[35] Cultivating a posture of wonder is akin to the patient work of waiting for bread to rise. It cannot be forced, cannot be conjured. It's really a work of bringing together enough resources and then hoping for the best. It's maddening in that way—bread making and wonder cultivating alike. So much of it is beyond our control and what is in our control is only so for a short while. But as with the imperfect gift of daily bread, this too is an invitation to be reconciled with our mortality. It is an invitation to remembrance that we are both brought into and being brought into full communion with God. Now and not yet. And such work is more often than we care to admit quiet and ordinary and seemingly dull. Unless, I think, we are mindful of where to look for excitement. Not in the fire or the thunderstorm or the earthquake, though they have their places too. But in the common, the repeated, the expected. In ordinary is miracle. It is as much miracle dough rises in a few hours as the sun once again cresting the horizon to herald a new day. This week, we will consider how to cultivate a discipline of wonder. At the same time, we'll discuss the rising part of bread making, the hands-off moment in which all you have control over is a few aspects of environment, then there is nothing more to do but wait and trust.

When you leave your dough to sit in gentle warmth for its first rise, you're giving it the needed room to generate flavor and to grow. The yeasty, salty sweet of bread comes from the slow alchemy of yeast feeding off the sugars in the dough. The robust shape comes from the carbon dioxide produced by the yeast as it feeds, which puffs up the loaf with intricate pockets of air.

(While there's a good deal written about what kind of yeast is best and whether or not fresh is the only way to go, I've never noticed a significant difference between fresh yeast and active dry, which is what most people have on hand or can find in the grocery store. In my opinion, the convenience of active dry yeast, which stays fresh for usually a year, if not more, outweighs the fickle fresh yeast that doesn't last beyond a handful of months.)

The rising process in total takes anywhere from an hour and a half to three hours. The timing is about temperature. The colder a space, the longer the rise. Bread is as temperamental as we tend to be, so it likes to keep in a space that is not too hot and not too cold. Ideally, this is just above room temperature, but most of us do not live in ideals. Since flavor is produced while our yeast feeds on the flour in the mixture and rise is yielded while the yeast releases carbon dioxide, if the dough is in too hot a space, the yeast releases gas too quickly and doesn't have enough time to feed, leaving our bread tasting bland. Alternatively, too long a rise in a cold space and the yeast runs out of food, turning bitter in flavor despite its robustness in form.

Typically, I'm able to get dough through its first rise, or through its bulk proof, as it is sometimes called, in just over two hours. That's the ideal in my current kitchen, which has concrete floors that trap the heat or the chill of the seasons. When my wife and I visit my parents, in a house that is open-planned and prone to cold, I set the bowl of dough to rise atop the running dryer in the laundry room. When it's the height of Texas summer, the dough is set low to the ground, typically on a space normally occupied by some of our wine glasses. Hot air rises, cold air lowers, so even in a warm apartment, keeping the dough low to the ground helps it not rise too quickly. If you have a free cabinet space in your kitchen near the floor, this is also a good option when it's too warm.

The rising process is the time of waiting, the time where it's good to take a short walk or read or answer that one email you never seem to get to. Thirty minutes in, we will turn and fold the dough gently to help it retain moisture and structure, but after that we back away for another stretch of time. How do you know when the rising is finished? When the dough has doubled in original size, the dough is ideal. By general rule, after turning the dough give it a look an hour in, then again a half hour later. If it looks like it needs a bit more time—in deep winter, mine tends to—wait another half hour. This is the most patient work we do in bread making, but it's the most rewarding. This is where effort is returned with taste and shape. We have put our best in, now we see what will come out.

If we are to talk about wonder—in ourselves, in the world, in others—we have to talk about our bodies. Our fear of flesh in Christianity has a long and colorful history, but it owes more to Greek philosophers than to the Bible. The Bible doesn't fear flesh, eating, drinking, sex, giving birth. It was the influence of ancient philosophy that taught early Christians to care only for their souls as if the soul were a separate thing from the body itself. Such heresy was known as Gnosticism and was condemned, but the impression of it lingers even today.

Scripture teaches us bodies are not shameful things. Scripture teaches us bodies are remarkable, beautiful, extraordinary things. The Song of Solomon, though apt, is not our only example. In the incarnation of Jesus, bodies are forever proclaimed to be good. Jesus does not shun the flesh, does not fear it. Jesus takes on flesh and by such flesh brings about the redemption of all flesh. Jesus tells us this body, this very body of his, is what brings about our reconciliation with God: "I am the living bread that came down from heaven. Whoever eats of this bread will live forever; and the bread that I will give for the life of the world is my flesh."[36] In light of this, could we ever reasonably argue God's displeasure with the physical if it was by the physical God brought us back to God's own self? I don't think we can. The incarnation of Jesus commends us to see all physical things as dear to the heart of God, welcomed by the very being of God, and all things of the body, all things the body experiences, to be meaningful, miracle, ordinary holiness. Gregory of Nyssa wrote of Jesus in his baptism that when Christ entered the waters he forever made them holy, that the waters we now enter for our own baptism are made holy because of Christ's entrance into them as well.[37] Everything Jesus does in the incarnation is a hallowing act, ordinary as it may seem to be. The incarnation is a rallying cry — our bodies are not sacks of flesh; they are bound up into the identity of God! There is no dividing the soul from the body in the same way there is no dividing Jesus from humanity after the incarnation.

Lest we further miss the point, the resurrection of Jesus is not a casual event. Jesus rises again in a body of flesh, not as an apparition. Jesus is a fully human person resurrected in a glorified and perfected body. A fleshy, physical, you-can-touch-it body. And we are becoming what Jesus is.

Curiously, there are things about the body of Jesus after the resurrection which may be surprising and strange to our normal imaginings of what perfected flesh should be like. Jesus can walk through walls, but he still has the scars of the cross. Jesus eats breakfast with the disciples, but he also can disappear, as he did after breaking bread with the disciples on the road to Emmaus. The fleshy body remains central, though, for without it there would be no Mary Magdalene clinging to Jesus when she first sees him or Thomas touching pierced flesh when he demands proof.[38]

God is not ashamed of our bodies. God is not ashamed of God's creation.

The old story tells us God the Creator called this world good. The entrance of sin into the creation is a disfigurement, but it will be healed. At the end of all things, Scripture does not say God's judgment is to destroy all the beauty of this place, but to make it new, to bring it fully into the presence of God. In Revelation, the heavenly Jerusalem is brought down to earth, not we up to it, breaking free of this physical world. God's eternal kingdom is irrevocably linked to where we are right this moment. As Saint Cyril of Jerusalem described the apocalypse, "The Lord rolls up the heavens, not that he may destroy them, but that he may raise them up again more beautiful."[39]

God takes pleasure in this creation, not just the creation that will be in the age to come.

God is already in the midst of us. God is already known here, even if only known in part.

God is not exclusively concerned with the spiritual, but with the whole of us, with the whole of the cosmos. The physical, the spiritual, the essence, and the being all blur. There is no distinction of these things to God. You are not a soul trapped in a body. You are not a body without spiritual connection. To be is to exist in a physical spiritual whirlwind without separation. We cannot be without physical. We cannot be without spiritual. This is the central message of the incarnation and the resurrection—God has come to redeem all of us, the whole of us along with the whole of creation. As Paul writes,

> For the creation waits with eager longing for the revealing of the [children] of God. For the creation was subjected to futility, not willingly, but because of him who subjected it, in hope that the creation itself will be set free from its bondage to corruption and obtain the freedom of the glory of the children of God.[40]

Understanding ourselves and this world as inseparable from the physical and the spiritual is called a sacramental view of creation.

A sacrament, singular, is a unique gift of God by which God assures us God is made known to us through it. We'll talk more specifically about sacraments near the end of this book; for now, it's important to clarify how we get to sacraments specifically—particular ways in which God says we might know God — is by the more general confession of the sacramental character of the universe.

A sacramental regard for the creation recognizes that because God desires to make God's own self known to us, there are infinite moments of revelation by the Holy Spirit that can happen in the midst of wilderness, along a path, in the breath-catching moment when we remember our God is the Creator. It's recognition we cannot take the world away from the One who made it. The Creator has formed a world that sings out God's workmanship. And if we are to believe Paul, it is not only ourselves but also our world that is being brought into the life of God.

Here is the invitation to wonder: God has come near to us, near to this universe, is making invitation to the whole to be brought back into union with God. As the theological philosopher David Bentley Hart describes it, "In the Christian God, the infinite is seen to be beautiful and so capable of being traversed by way of the beautiful."[41] Hart is saying because God is the infinite, the all, the everything around us, and God is beautiful, one of the ways in which we draw nearer to God is through beauty. When we recognize the beauty of what God has made we recognize something of the beauty of God. We journey the infinite space between us and God. Yet because God is both beyond us and near us, we find the distance itself is full of God's presence, for in God we live and move and have our being. The discipline of wonder is a way of encountering beauty, seeking it out, and drawing closer to the infinite source of all beauty.

We are roasting split peaches pressed flush against browned butter in a cast iron pan. There's mascarpone and goat cheese being beaten together with a bit of sugar and I have the ceremonial task of individuating the sage leaves. We have each ended up here by chance. On the edge of a city in a rented house, schedules overlapping, about twenty of us make ever-expanding and constricting circles of conversation. These roast peaches are happy accident, pulled together from three different grocery runs, leftovers of sporadic feast. It's nearing midnight and the music — guitars, on the porch and inside — weaves us together. We dress the peaches in their pan juices, teetering on mismatched and chipped plates, crowned with the cream mixture, finished with a leaf of sage.

Sage is an herb of knowing. In ancient times, Greeks and Romans strongly associated it with prophetic wisdom, imparted when the leaves were burned as incense in temples. Folklore holds if you put a leaf of sage with a wish written on it under your pillow and over three nights dream about it, it will come true. I don't know about all of that, but when I walk out of the kitchen with a few plates balanced on arms, pass them into waiting hands, take a seat in the circle, and accept an offered drink, there is a sort of knowing. It's a knowing of space, an awareness of body. It's a knowing about the people that form this circle, that they are a people of devotion and intention. The peaches are as sticky-messy as our lives, a metaphor that would be trite if it weren't achingly true. We eat them unabashedly, interjecting humor and sympathy and observation between mouthfuls. We are weary, but we did not know it until we were here, where the music flames out into the night and the wonder never stops.

There comes a moment when we are singing hymns. Old things. Would-be-forgotten things. For some of us this is a return, circling back to our roots. This is healing work. There are survivors here of evil costumed in the holy. When they sing it's defiance, resistance, a means to chase away the dark. Songs get in you, like heat and chill I suppose, and when we hear a few chords linked tender and sure, the words come back and prove to still be true:

> This is my Father's world.
> O let me ne'er forget,
> That though the wrong seems oft so strong,
> God is the ruler yet.

It's an odd thing, how we forget a part of ourselves to only find it again. We think we know ourselves well, but then something surfaces in us demanding attention and we are not sure from where it has come. In this circle we know a part of ourselves again. We know a part that is stigmatized and hard to look at, sometimes embarrassing, sometimes painful. We drag bits of peach and sage across plates to take up every last drop of sauce. It is loud, it is pronounced, it is bright—but it is peaceful. It is still. The loudness is rootedness. The knowing is peace making. The whole of it is awe, wonderment.

> This is my Father's world:
> The battle is not done:
> Jesus who died shall be satisfied
> and earth and Heav'n be one.

Understanding the world as sacramental liberates us from the need to lay hold of God. Sometimes, we hitch our faith to a falling star of excitement that flames out well before we realize it has. Sacramental perspective tenderly reminds us God does not need invitation to inhabit a space or to be present—God already is. God, in whom "we live and move and have our being" is already with us, has already drawn near.[42]

Ancient philosophers of geometry and physics described the movement of the planets to be ordered in such a way that it was as if they were set to song, calling it the music of the spheres. The music was not literal, but descriptive of the great order of the universe, slowly keeping its course. God as the great conductor of the orchestra of creation is not a new image. Perhaps because music is both ordered and free, guided but permissive. It fills a space, flows through and around and in. We are the players of our instruments, our lives, and they can follow the direction of the conductor or they can deviate. There is patience for the disharmony of this imperfect orchestra, for as Peter reminds us, "The Lord is not slow to fulfill his promise as some count slowness, but is patient toward you, not wishing that any should perish, but that all should reach repentance."[43] God leads this orchestra of a cosmos on to some unknown time, some unknown end, except that in the end there will be and will remain harmony. God is already present to us, near us, with us, and, for many, in us.

We are in the process of entering into harmony with not only God but also each other. Someday, not too long from now, we shall all be connected, vibrant, free. What a wonder.

Thirty minutes into the first rise, we fold our dough.

Folding dough is tender work, requiring as much gentleness in hands as was demanded of us while kneading. Sure, but gentle. As before, we're going slow to keep our gluten strong, retaining the hard work of the structure it has been making for us. All you need to do is wet your hands and your dough spatula. Run the spatula around the edges of your dough to lift it free from sticking to the sides of the bowl, then put your spatula down. Using your hands, gently bring up and over the part of the dough furthest from you back to yourself, making the first fold. Turn the bowl a quarter and repeat, then turn it another quarter and do the same. Going slow, letting the dough stretch itself without forcing it, will ensure our previous efforts to give the dough the best possible conditions will be rewarded. Recover the dough and return it to where it was.

Once again, we wait. After an hour, take a peek at the dough. You will notice the seams created when we folded it are disappearing, if not already gone. Gluten slowly brings equilibrium back to the mass and provides us a once again silken form. Wet your hands and touch the top of the dough, testing the firmness. If the dough feels a bit dense, give it another fifteen minutes and then check it again. If it feels particularly dense, consider moving it to a warmer space and check it again in fifteen minutes. Allowing for more time to rise isn't a problem so long as we are mindful of the dough and don't forget about it. As was mentioned when we were kneading, there is a gift of imperfection in this work.

When the dough feels a bit firm but unsure underneath your touch, when it holds the imprints of your fingers slightly, it is ready for division and forming. This is the process that remains a marvel to me, how bread slowly becomes itself with so little of our input when it comes down to it. We have only brought in means to make, but it is the dough itself that comes alive and into its own. Similar, I think, to the Spirit. The Spirit takes the whole of us, the assembled being, and shapes us into something increasingly looking like Jesus. That process is, at times, less about our doing and more about our patience, with ourselves as much with the world, our surprise when we discover kindness or sincerity we did not think to have. Suddenly we are filled with love that was not previously our habit. Suddenly we are hopeful in the midst of despair. We are motivated to learn the name of the person working the checkout line at the grocery store; we take a neighbor's trash to the curb. Small things and great things alike. When we are observant, we are inclined to hear the Spirit prompt us.

This is the great mystery, I think, how God realizes in us the purposes of our being.

Nothing about that can be forced. We can only lay hold of the best we have to offer, sometimes the best we have at the time, and see what is to be made. One day we look around and realize we've already been gracious for years without paying attention to it. One day we find a knowing in our hands when the dough is perfectly done.

The discipline of wonder is, fundamentally, a discipline of curiosity, a desire to see anew the too-familiar.

Do you know the depths to which Jesus loves you?

Do you know he loves every bit of you, every inch of flesh and weird-shaped pinky and runny nose?

Do you know that Jesus calls our bodies good because Jesus has a body too?

Do you know life in God means a life full of God's presence not just in your soul but in the very midst of your being?

Do you know this Gospel? Do you know this good news?

Isn't this the best news of all? Our bodies are God's delight. Our bodies are not shameful. Our bodies are not the guilty ones.

Redemption of sin is not just for our souls. It is for the very everything of us.

Similar to intercessory prayer, the work of wondering is one without much use for direction. It would be easy and appropriate to commission you into simply going forth into the world for the week and seeing what you find. But I know practical work is helpful, so let me offer some guiding ideas for the week ahead. I've put together a little list, of which you may take or leave however much you want. Give yourself permission this week to go slow, to walk tender, to take in only as much as you are compelled to do. Slow down. Notice. Be. Marvel.

- Become unreachable for the week. Delete every social-media app from your phone, answer only email you have to, don't text or call unless necessary.

- Go on a walk and pay attention to the world around you. Notice. See how the leaves on the trees are formed, the color of the dirt, the stretch of the skyline. If your walk does not take you into a space you would normally identify as beautiful, look to see if you can find something about it that is. Seek out the goodness of the creation. Wonder at it and in turn give thanks and praise to God for it.

- Spend some time with someone you know well and practice noticing something new about them. Perhaps it is something to share, something tender or funny. Seek the way God is making God's own self known to you in the face of another person.

- Dance in your kitchen. Put on the music you're embarrassed you own and dance. Feel your body in motion and press into it, come to know it anew. Be grateful for it, for the weight of it and the shape of it and the flesh of it. Celebrate your body in the presence of God by dancing free, unencumbered by pretense.

- Pick up a collection of poems and read one each morning. Turn over a line or two over the course of the day. Notice how poetry shapes the posture of your heart toward the world around you. Consider how it helps you hear or see or know something you had not known before.

- Practice silence and stillness. Sit on your porch or in your living room or under a tree, and be quiet for a half hour. Don't force anything here. This isn't meditation per se. If you have things to think about, think about them, but also think about them only as far as they will be thought and then free yourself from them. Get still and pay attention, offer everything back to God.

- Don't do anything outside of attending church and spending time with your family on a Sunday. Give over to God the trust that time is not in your control, that you are unnecessary to keep the world in motion, that God will provide the time and the space to accomplish all that needs doing.

For This Week

DISCIPLINE

- Take up some of the ideas from page 91 for this week.

BAKE

- Pay close attention this week to the rising process. What do you notice? What smells do you detect? Changes in state?

- When you taste the bread, what stands out to you? Salt? Sugar? Yeast? Do any of these flavors pull you into contemplation?

- How does letting the dough rise in one part of your kitchen or the other change it?

ASK

- When was the last time you met the presence of God in a place you did not expect it?

- How does cultivating time for stillness and wonder in your life shape other parts of it? Does wonder help you feel more present even in chaotic moments?

- What are you noticing anew? What is taking your attention this week? What is drawing you in?

Forming: Rootedness

The less communal our lives become, the less communal our expectations of our religious environments. We forget the countless stories of the gospels in which community is the space into which God comes to us. We forget the early church and its fierce rootedness and commitment to the community. We resist the need for one another, out of hurt or fear or pride, and make faith the sum of our own thoughts, our own beliefs, our own confessions. Maybe it comes from a good intention, a reaction away from treating salvation as an abstract idea for a community, not for individuals like you and me.

The path is about balance as much as it is about journey. The path teaches us there is good in seeking out those who walk with us and those who have walked before us. Those gone before pass back directions, suggestions, word about whether there is a deviation in the road, a storm on the horizon. In Christianity, we might refer to these journeyers gone before us as the cloud of witnesses or, to encompass both their lives and their work, we might call it the tradition.

The idea of religious tradition is sometimes unsettling, stirring up gloomy renditions of Latin services or incense or a host of images tied to requirements and rules and a laundry list of *can'ts* and *thou may nots*. It's true, not all tradition is good. Tradition has more than once been used for an earthly denying of the abundance of God's love for all people; but, incidents of misuse should not prevent us from the abundance it could provide.

In recent years, more and more churches are seeing the great wealth of the Christian tradition, or what I like to think of as our shared history, our rootedness. Across denominational lines, evangelicals are discovering the ways in which the ancient and premodern church sought relationship with God, how it wrestled through difficult questions of meaning and existence, and how the marking of ordinary things as sacred developed a holistic, wonder-filled engagement with the natural world. Movements like the Practice, hosted in the Chapel of Willow Creek, or the reformation work of the Anglican Church in North America, draw upon charismatic, evangelical, and historic expressions of faithful Christian witness. We are increasingly opening ourselves to the possibility of the authority and wisdom of those gone before us. We are considering the vastness of Christian experience to extend beyond the measure of what we ourselves can say we have seen, have heard, have known—and this can only be for our good.

Tradition forms us, feeds us, gives us roots. It shapes us as we strive in partnership with the Holy Spirit to embody the likeness of Jesus. But the work is long, complex, unending. It's an old speculation by the church that in heaven we will still learn and create and grow in who we are, for if God is infinite, then there is infinity to explore and come to understand. I am comforted that there's always but one more thing to discover and to know about God. I'm comforted there are so many ways and kinds of knowing. Some knowing is in the hands touching bread, some in the work of the field, some in the pages of words penned millennia before. Still more kinds, still more ways, too many to count. God seeks a plurality of experience with us, a shifting kaleidoscope of encounter. The diversity of the creation is itself testimony to this. As the discipline of wonder encouraged us to see, there is always something new, no matter how old, right in front of us. We press on into newness, glory to glory, as the apostle Paul said, and just when we think we've reached the end, there's a tilt in the earth and we find it continues on. This is the gift of rootedness: we open ourselves to learn from one another in and across time, to discover God anew day by day. This week, we'll be considering a few ways to dip our feet into the ocean of Christian witness, as well as the patient work of the initial forming of our loaves of bread.

"What do you have that you did not receive? And if you did receive it, why do you boast as if you had not received it?"[44] Paul asks this of the Christians in Corinth, who had presented themselves as if they were without need of instruction or guidance from those gone before them. The apostle soundly dismisses the notion, reminding them the gospel is a received thing, passed from one to another, gifted from one to another, so without community there would be no sharing. None of us are brought to faith in isolation. We are handed the things preserved by those who have walked the path before us, who serve as guides for where we are to go next.

I am mindful of the Exodus story—*who will tell their story?*—of why we read Scripture carefully, because we are in a line of faithful people who were told thousands of years ago their work was to hand down the story of God and the people of God. Such is the command of Deuteronomy 6:

> And these words that I command you today shall be on your heart. You shall teach them diligently to your children, and shall talk of them when you sit in your house, and when you walk by the way, and when you lie down, and when you rise. You shall bind them as a sign on your hand, and they shall be as frontlets between your eyes. You shall write them on the doorposts of your house and on your gates.[45]

The Scripture itself is a kind of tradition, handed down to us generation after generation. But Scripture is not the only tradition out of which the Holy Spirit speaks. The faithful witness of the early church, of those gone before us after the last pages of Scripture were penned, is a way the Spirit speaks to us even today. As an Anglican, I find my church holds the deep conviction Scripture is primary in our formation, then we venture into waters fed by three streams comprising our identity: catholic, evangelical, and charismatic. We are catholic, that is universal, in our belief in the sacramental nature of the world and our commitment to the larger Christian tradition. We are evangelical in our belief that the gospel is an urgent matter, needing to be preached in all times and places. We are charismatic in our belief that the Holy Spirit is alive and dynamic, at work in us and our communities, leading us forward in miraculous and ordinary ways.

Oftentimes we, Anglicans or otherwise, do not struggle with being evangelical or charismatic. We struggle with tradition. We struggle with aspects of religion we believe to be more about man than about God. Yet the Bible does not resist tradition. The Bible welcomes it. The Bible commends to us God's appreciation of our reverence, our desire to do things well, to speak of God well, to fill the spaces in which we say God has come to dwell with the beauty God deserves. Being a temple of the Holy Spirit is not only about us but also about the larger witness of the faithful gone before us, who would offer back perspective and conviction and discernment of how to make the interior spaces of our lives beautiful for God. Tradition need not be suspicious if we are mindful of its fundamental purpose: to root us, center us back again and again on the wonder and awe of God. Moreover, tradition is also not exclusively formal, high church, Roman Catholic or Eastern Orthodox. Tradition includes Pentecostal voices, Italian mystics, slave spirituals and hymns, and countless other diverse perspectives and testimonies. Our unity is not found in our complete agreement, but in our connection to one another in Jesus. (Along the same lines as the idea of connection we consider with intercession.) The difference of views, approaches, and understandings are a gift to us. They allow us new ways to worship God, new ways to see God's world, new ways to abide in the seasons when God seems far off.

Study is perhaps the most common suggestion made when one begins the discipline of rootedness. Easy, because what it usually requires of you is just a bit of reading. Daunting, because most people consider the writings of famous Christians who lived long ago to be inaccessible to the modern reader. What we often forget is many early Christian writings were for the benefit of everyday people — they are commentaries on Scripture, meditations on daily life as faithful believers, reflections on God's nearness to us.

Too, expanding our understanding of the Christian tradition is not limited to the distant past. Our broadened perspective should include communities foreign to us, especially contemporary communities. As a white male who is able-bodied and middle class, I should actively seek out the perspectives of people of color, women, persons with disabilities, and others whose experiences may not align with my own. The diversity of the church is its beauty and strength. An active engagement with diversity keeps us in a healthy perspective: we are not the center of the faith and our experience is not infallible. Jesus is the center of our faith and Jesus is not confined to any particular narrative we find the most comforting. Jesus comes often to us in the words of someone we would never expect. Engaging different perspectives about God is needed to remain teachable, remain amazed, remain curious.

In the appendix of this book, you'll find a list of suggested texts I have found extremely helpful in beginning a life of Christian study. The beauty of such work is you need not commit more time to it than you are able. Some seasons I manage only a page a day of something, but the gift of words from a fellow believer, gone before or still walking beside, helps me fix my eyes on the larger story of God's work in this world, not only my place within it.

What on earth could rootedness to Christian tradition have to do with forming dough?

Dividing dough is an unceremonious task with no room for pretense. There's a good deal of flopping and flipping and hoping for the best. Let that be a welcome to you instead of a hindrance. Accept the necessary task of disorder. There will be flour on your kitchen floor. There will be sticky dough clinging to your elbow. These things are unavoidable but these things are also the stuff of real, ordinary, miraculous life. Like being formed by the tradition. You'll read or hear something and feel yourself split a bit, something push out that surprises you, and what was sure becomes not-so-sure. This is a part of life too. This too is miracle. But back to the dough.

To divide our dough, we first sprinkle a bit of flour over its risen top. Next, using our dough spatula, we run a quick circle around its parameter to free it from the sides of the bowl. Then, quickly overturn the bowl onto your kitchen counter. You should hear a satisfying thud, the dough released onto the countertop. If you don't, give the bottom of the overturned bowl a hearty whack, which should do the trick. Remove the bowl and you are face-to-face with a sticky, petulant mass. Flour your hands, your dough scraper—as noted in the recipe, this time you're using your stainless-steel scraper with the cutting edge, not the flexible scraper we have used up to this point—and the countertop where you will be working with the dough. Using direct and certain pressure, cut the dough in half with your dough scraper, ensuring the blade makes contact with the countertop below your dough, making the cut clean. As soon as you have cut, use the scraper to divide the two portions of dough from each other by several inches.

Because we're making boules—a French word literally meaning *bowl*—our shaping work is simple. We're making round loaves, so all you need is patience. We shape our dough twice: the first time imperfectly, just to get used to the idea of the final form it will take on; the second time specifically, confirming the structure we'll see when the bread finally comes back to us out of the oven.

For the first shaping, we fold in a similar form as we did when the bread was still rising. Our purpose here is to put some tension in the structure of the dough. Simple, steady, decisive motion is what is called for here. Pull the part of the dough furthest from you back to yourself, making the first fold. Using your dough spatula, turn the dough a quarter and repeat, then turn it a quarter again and do the same. Finally, using the dough spatula underneath your package of dough, flip the dough over so the seams are now face down on the countertop. Do the same to the other mass of dough, leaving several inches between each.

That's it. Sprinkle a little flour over their tops and cover them with a kitchen towel. Let the dough rest anywhere from fifteen minutes to an hour, depending on what kind of time you have. This rest allows us to fold the dough one last time and keep the tension in it without tearing the surface, which helps us make big bread without thick fault lines or shredded gluten.

This part of bread making is unnecessary if we are only concerned with utility. Technically speaking, this dough could just go right into the oven and a very edible baked thing would be produced. The work here is about shape, structure, and quality. I think of our rootedness to the Christian tradition similarly. We can go just fine on our own in this world without much more than the Holy Spirit and the Scripture, but the end result doesn't have the same kind of beauty of form and substance. Tradition roots us. It is for our good, our glorification, that others who have encountered God pass along notes of the exchange, keep a living record of what has been seen or heard or revealed. Shaping dough is akin to "working out our faith with fear and trembling"; it's just the latter doesn't need to be done alone.[46]

The most formative discipline of rootedness in my own life has been observing the church year, which is sometimes called the liturgical year. The church year is a way of thinking about time in a spiritual sense, not a secular one. We follow a rhythm of calendar focused exclusively on Jesus and the work of God's redemption and commissioning of us. The church year is fixed firmly in a pattern of Scripture so, like Scripture, there is something fresh to encounter each time it is returned to, no matter how many times we do. As I mentioned when we discussed *lectio divina*, I follow the daily lectionary in my Bible reading. The daily lectionary aligns itself with the church year, the readings focusing me on a particular theme of God's love, mercy, and justice appropriate to the season.

The church year—and to clarify, we're following the Western church year in this book, the Eastern Orthodox calendar is a bit different—is divided into seasons and days, each with particular emphasis and focus, but all centered around the life of Jesus. The year does not begin on January 1, but four Sundays before Christmas Day, with the season called Advent. Advent focuses us in two directions at the same time: we look back with the expectation we have for the coming of Jesus in the incarnation; we look forward with the expectation we have for the coming of Jesus again in the apocalypse. Advent is a time to get the metaphorical house of our hearts ready. We figuratively sweep the floors, but we also buy the wine. A Guest of great importance is coming, so we plan accordingly. Advent, unlike Lent, is not a season of fasting. Advent is a season of clearing out and stocking up, preparing for Jesus.

On Christmas Day, we begin a twelve-day feast that runs from the twenty-fifth to the sixth of January. Christmas is the great and triumphant celebration of Jesus coming to us in the incarnation. In Christmas, we celebrate and mark the arrival of our Lord and his nearness, his knowing of us and abiding with us. Then, on the sixth of January, we enter Epiphany. Epiphany begins with telling the story of the magi coming to honor Jesus, which is the first clear example we have in the Scriptures of the Gentiles encountering the incarnate God. The weeks that follow feature gospel readings tracing the way Jesus slowly made himself known as God to the disciples. Epiphany is a season of revelation, encountering God in surprises. It varies in length, dependent on the date of Easter, but usually lasts seven to nine weeks.

After Epiphany, we enter Lent, which begins on Ash Wednesday, forty days, Sundays excluded, before Easter. Ash Wednesday is the day we receive the ashen cross upon our foreheads, a reminder that we are but dust and to dust we will return. Lent is a season of fasting. Unlike Advent, we are not readying the house of our hearts as much as we are renovating it, getting rid of the old and useless. Sundays are the exception in this season, for Sunday, the day Jesus resurrected, is always a feast. (We'll be discussing fasting and feasting more in the coming chapters.) Lent focuses us on the ways in which we are in need of Jesus, the great extent of our sin and its effects on the world and ourselves, and reminds us of our great hope, which is only found in God.

At the end of Lent, we enter Passiontide, or Holy Week, the week that culminates with Maundy Thursday, Good Friday, and finally Holy Saturday. This week brings us into the cosmic timelessness of the historical death of our God, forces us to reckon with the absurd beauty of God's willingness to be faithful to us even to the point of death. It is a week marked with sorrow and tenderness and the depths of hopelessness. And then, with great triumph, we are brought out of the darkness into the resplendent light of Easter. The great feast of Easter is not, as some think, only one day. Eastertide is a season fifty days long, a time of feasting and celebration and joy and merriment. Death is defeated! Jesus is alive! Eastertide is a season of champagne and late nights and foretastes of the heavenly party here and now. Forty days into Eastertide we mark the ascension of Jesus back into heaven, and on the fiftieth day we celebrate the Sunday of Pentecost, when the Holy Spirit came upon the believers and empowered them to do the good work God had in store. Pentecost is the climax of our being, the moment when it became possible for us to be like Jesus, to be shaped and refined into his image and likeness.

After Pentecost, we enter the season of Ordinary Time II, sometimes called Kingdom Time, the longest of all the seasons. Ordinary Time is the season in which we are mindful we have been sent out into this world by Jesus to announce the kingdom of God is at hand, has come near, is now. Ordinary Time is a time of mindfulness, of reminding us the work of faith is often common, ordinary, seemingly unremarkable. This is the season in which the readings focus on the life of the early church, its struggles to be faithful and in what manner faithfulness should pattern itself. Ordinary Time is a gift of praising the common life of belief, the season in which the planted things of faith take root, are given time to blossom and grow before it all begins again with Advent.

It's a lot, I know, but there's such a joy in being shaped by it. The easiest way to observe the church year in your own life is to follow the daily lectionary for your Bible reading. Following the daily cycle will bring you into the mindset of observing the seasons. There are a number of resources for thinking about and observing the church year in your family too, a curated list of which you will find on pages 167–68 of this book.

Each season of the church year is akin to each careful shaping of the dough. You don't always know what will come of it, what will surprise you is what has turned from seamed mess into smoothed crust. But as we find our rootedness in the larger story of our faith, we find God has been quietly shaping us over and over, pulling us and stretching us into a gentle form. The church year, like our steady hands, brings structure and shape where we would have wandered, gives a sense of connection to those gone before us on the path, reminds us to leave direction behind for those who will come after.

The whole cohort of us is spread around the apartment on deadline. It's the night before our last paper of the semester is due, and we have ended up in this space in varying levels of preparedness. Some are nearly finished, some just beginning. Most had arrived by noon, and though I still had another five pages to write, I spent the afternoon wandering in and out of the rooms asking people if they would like something to eat. There was frenzy in those first hours, the graduate-school panic, but by first dark, about half past six, a lull has settled over us. We are not despairing, but resigned. Whatever is turned out shall be turned out and there no longer seems much cause to fret. On impulse that morning I had baked an unleavened piece of flatbread, remnant of a bit of flour and oil leftover from a dinner party the week before. This piece of flatbread held no significance or interest until the first dark, when we looked at each other and realized it was too late to walk back into town and make a church service.

It is Maundy Thursday.

There is conversation, brief, about what is to be done. We are a mix of beliefs, convictions, traditions, rootedness, but we all seem to agree something should be done. At the ninth hour we gather in the kitchen around the barren table, the space where more than once I have fed these faces, set aglow by four candles flickering around the room. (The bruise on the table still pulsates, still feels warm to the touch.) What happens next is hard to recount, a blend of Christian response. Some of us read from King James and some cross themselves. Some pray in tongues and some read from *The Message*. The diversity is unified in this one thing of flatbread and, after some compromise, a bit of wine. Someone calls them body and blood.

Someone breaks the first piece. Someone passes the cup. Someone does not receive. Someone offers a blessing.

It is a strange night, as Maundy Thursday always is. We mark the gift of Jesus to know him through ordinary creatures of bread and wine, but tonight we do more than this, for we mark the gift of the diversity of Christian faith. We pronounce good the different ways we come to this place where we say Jesus is made known. We live out and into and through a unity only found in the depths of Jesus. Here, we are one. We join the thousands gone before us and the thousands who are to come. We are all met at that table by the Jesus who says by these things we may know him. He dwells in us and we in him, different and particular and unique and yet, remarkably, miraculously, in this the same.

Some seasons of my life are so chaotic or so boring, I turn to the gift of rootedness found in fixed-hour prayer, meaning you pray at specific times of the day. The approach was developed by the same monastic communities who took up *lectio divina* as part of their daily practice. Often, psalms and hymns made up the bulk of the guided prayers with a handful of places for personal intercessions and intentions. This started much earlier than the monastics, though.

When the Israelites were in exile and the first temple had been destroyed, they developed a culture of fixed-hour services in which the Torah and psalms were to be read. The mention of *sacrifices of praise* in the Scripture is because animal sacrifices could no longer be made to God in absence of the first temple. Though Christians recognized the atoning death of Jesus as once and for all making sufficient sacrifice to God, the practice of fixed-hour worship did not end. Over the centuries, many forms have emerged. Some are specific and rigorous, some are loose and free-flowing. All share the desire to be mindful and present to Jesus, to keep him close in all things that we do.

I came into being an Anglican in college, after being raised, happily, as a Southern Baptist, a journey I detail at length in my first book, *Tables in the Wilderness: A Memoir of God Found, Lost, and Found*

Again. As an Anglican, it is part of my custom to pray through the morning and evening prayers found in the Book of Common Prayer, greeting and bidding the day farewell by focusing on Jesus. Other traditions are more elaborate, incorporating morning and evening to start, but adding several other times of the day. This may include the five Major Hours, points in the day where lengthy, guided intercession is made. Others recognize Minor Hours too, times between the Major Hours, smaller pauses of intercession and focus. Fixed-hour prayer roots us to see the world as a place where God intimately dwells with and in us. The day is framed with Jesus.

Fixed-hour prayer is sometimes referred to as the liturgy of the hours or the Divine Office. What is often difficult for people who desire to take on this practice of prayer is the logistics. So, if you are interested in stepping into such a practice—and I do hope you will consider it—let me offer some guidelines of where and how to start.

First of all, begin simply. Find something like a copy of the Book of Common Prayer (1979), either physical or digital, and consider following the morning and evening prayer forms within it. (Check to be sure you're using the form for individuals, not for a congregation, or you may find it odd that you're being asked to refer to people who are not present or that you are beginning every prayer with *we*.)

Second, if the rhythm of morning and evening prayer appeals to you, consider looking into some of the recent books that have been published, along with smartphone apps. Phyllis Tickle has done a great service to the church with her Divine Hours series, Shane Claiborne and Jonathan Wilson-Hartgrove produced the helpful *Common Prayer*, and Scot McKnight's *Praying with the Church* is a fine, excellent place to begin. Personally, I use a small breviary from Lancelot Andrewes Press, called *The Monastic Diurnal*, which follows an older form of the daily office that would have been common among monastics in Britain in the late Middle Ages. A search for *Divine Hours* or *Divine Office* or *liturgy of the hours* on the Apple App Store produces a number of helpful options, all of good quality and, from best I can tell, beginner friendly.

Third, be patient and be present. Fixed-hour prayer, along the lines of the Examen and *lectio*, is a labor of focus. God desires intimacy with you, so it's okay if you read the wrong prayer or read morning prayer at 9:00 p.m. It will happen—it still happens to me!—and that's not so bad. Somehow God still comes into the midst of us and says, *I am here.*

I am learning, still, for that to be enough for me.

It's enough to be rooted. To be shaped. To be guided. Then, miracle, to see what polished form I someday take.

For This Week

DISCIPLINE

- Take three days this week to practice fixed-hour prayer, even if just in the morning and evening. Use the forms found in the 1979 Book of Common Prayer or whatever prayer book or rubric is appropriate to you.

- Take two days this week to study for about twenty minutes. This might be picking up a copy of Athanasius's *On the Incarnation* or one of the other texts listed in the appendix of this book. Spend a little time working through it, slow and careful, and see what the Spirit quickens in you. Or perhaps it's finding a theologically rich podcast, like *On Being*, to listen to and reflect on what you hear.

- Follow the daily lectionary readings for the Scripture appropriate to the season of church year. Notice how the rhythm of passages comment on one another, and ask the Spirit to help you see what about the season is being communicated to you.

BAKE

- Feel how the dough has changed, how the gas made by the yeast has lifted it. Notice the lightness and the density.

- Practice feeling the weight of your own hands on the dough, noticing the point where command turns to too much pressure. Sense the lightness of you as you work.

- Spend some time thinking about how bread making might become a tradition in your own family to be passed down or passed alongside. Perhaps it's to your children, your parents, your friends.

ASK

- What are the traditions of Christianity that are the most meaningful to you personally? Why?

- What are some of your big questions about God? How have they changed over years or how have some remained? What do answers look like to those questions—a feeling, a knowing, a trusting? Is it a question that can even be answered?

- What traditions in Christianity make you the most uncomfortable? How have you wrestled with the discomfort and what have you learned? Are you still wrestling? Still uncomfortable?

Last Form, Last Rise: Remembrance

These past weeks we have focused on cultivating interior habits of heart that put us in larger relationship with the world. What these practices open us to is the broadness by which God comes to meet us. Now we consider the good work of remaining open, of keeping ourselves willing to encounter God anew even in the times when all else seems dull. There are seasons of life we all journey through at different times, but we all will know a winter here and there, sometimes a winter of years, a winter of months.

Near the end of winter in Scotland, on that path in that wood, things begin to change. It's a slow shift, so gradual you could miss it if you weren't looking for it. It's not the melting of the snow, though its absence leaves a stark impression on the mind. It's something after that, a first peeking blade of grass or a verdant streak pushing forth from a tree limb. Spring comes quietly to this wood, the gentle unfurling of new life. You don't notice it, not really, until you hear the water of the river stirring again, a sound you had forgotten in the months of absence and a sound you find hard to place when first hearing it again. But the sound quickens you, stirs an old memory of not so long ago, walking this path with someone and talking about something. Time collapses for a moment, and you are not in secular time, moving ever forward, but caught up into godly time, spiritual time, where past and present and future coexist in the fallow of memory. If not the sound of the water, then the scent of the first blossoms or the sight of the stone path along the riverbank, once again emerging after the sleep of snow draped across it. Such ordinary things—wonder-filled things, as we have considered—are signs to us. Signs of things that once were or perhaps signs of things that will be. Or both.

That's the thing about memory. Its work is at once tied intimately to the past and yet it remains directive of the future. Memory gives us language when words fail in the present. Memory offers us the means to make sense of the now. Repeatedly in Scripture, God commands the people to remember and to pass the memory on. Remember God is faithful. Remember God is good. This week, we will consider the discipline of remembrance, how it can easily be incorporated into our daily lives. We'll also discuss the last bit of work to be done before our bread, at long last, goes to rest in our oven.

One of the most common images in the early pages of the Old Testament is the altar.

Particularly in Genesis and Exodus, altars serve as constructed places of remembrance, signifying an intersection of humans and God. Altars are built as signs of covenant making, surety of God's work. For instance, when Abraham has journeyed into "the land to the place at Shechem, to the oak of Moreh" and God tells Abraham his descendants will possess the territory, Abraham builds an altar to mark the promise.[47] *Shechem* means "shoulder" and *Moreh* means "teacher." Abraham literally builds an altar, a sign of remembrance of the promise made to him, in the land where he has come to both rely on the strength of God—the shoulder—and the direction of God—the teacher. Consider too the altar upon which Abraham believed he would have to sacrifice his only son, Isaac. When God intervenes and provides a substitute for the sacrifice, the altar becomes a place of remembrance that it is God who will provide, who will rescue, who will save. Though not explicitly an altar, a similar intention is seen after Jacob dreams of the ladder coming down from heaven upon which angels ascend and descend, and God reminds Jacob that God is the God of his father and his father's father. Jacob erects a pillar in the space and calls it Bethel, which means "house of God."

Earlier we discussed the building of the tabernacle, how God called a specific group of people, those who were wise-hearted, to create the art for the space. Altars were a part of the tabernacle, along with dozens of other items carefully described in the last half of Exodus. What is striking is how particularly attached to the creation our early ancestors were, how God does not deter them from this affinity, but confirms and meets them within it. As Scripture continues to unfold, we repeatedly see God willingly making God's own self known in particular spaces and in particular ways attached to the physical experience of the creation. God does not only consider the natural creation to be good. God also identifies the artistry of humans to be of benefit in proclaiming God's nearness and promises.

The New Testament does not abandon this notion. When Jesus comes to the woman at the well in John 4, we are told it is Jacob's well, which biblical scholars believe to be the site of one of the altars Jacob constructed called El-Elohe-Israel, *God, the God of Israel*. At this well in Samaria, which by name specifically identifies Israel, not Samaria, as who God has called God's own, a Samaritan woman confronts a Hebrew Jesus, demanding to know where it is appropriate to worship God. Samaritans were former Jews whose bloodline had intermarried with surrounding pagans. The Jews despised them so much for this ancient offense, it was common for a Jew to walk around Samaria rather than go through it. Yet Samaritans believed they were still part of the children of God's promise, and they called Jacob their ancestor as much as the Jews did. Forbidden to worship in Jerusalem, however, the Samaritans were left to try and seek the God of Israel on their own terms. The woman's question to Jesus is quite telling. She is asking the Jewish Jesus if he will recognize validity in how she, a Samaritan, worships God. "Our fathers worshiped on this mountain," she says, "But you say that in Jerusalem is the place where people ought to worship."[48] Jesus replies,

> Woman, believe me, the hour is coming when neither on this mountain nor in Jerusalem will you worship the Father. You worship what you do not know; we worship what we know, for salvation is from the Jews. But the hour is coming, and is now here, when the true worshipers will worship the Father in spirit and truth, for the Father is seeking such people to worship him. God is spirit, and those who worship him must worship in spirit and truth.[49]

At a well named by Jacob to be the place where the God of Israel is present, the same God of Israel, now incarnate, comes to an outcast and says she is still a child of God. The well in the place of El-Elohe-Israel is no longer only a well of remembrance of God's giving of the land to Jacob, but is now a sign of how God has come to give living water to all who will receive it, regardless of who they are. The well-naming God as the God of Israel becomes the well where all may come to be grafted into the family of God, brothers and sisters with Jesus. Space, places, altars, wells—signs of God's intersection with us are vastly important if we believe the physical world itself is important. The good of the discipline of remembrance is that it teaches us the power of icons, objects in the world that pronounce to us reminders of God's goodness, God's might, God's holiness, God's love. Icons like Jacob's well, like altars in the wilderness, remind us of who God has revealed God's own self to be to us, to those gone before us, and for the shaping of imagination and memory of those who shall come after us.

Icons, from the word εἰκών in the Greek, prounced just like we pronounce *icon* and meaning "image," had difficulties in the formation of the early church. Though received favorably by some, the physical-world-fearing early writers of the faith were nervous that pictorial images of Jesus, Mary, apostles, saints, and angels would cause idolatry, the picture being worshiped instead of elevating thoughts to contemplation of the thing pictured. The criticism came out of a deep desire to honor the commandment to not make for oneself a graven image. This objection was contested, however, when the rest of the passage was considered, in which God commands detailing the cherubim and other heavenly creatures in building the elements of the tabernacle. Speculation shifted even further in favor of icons as people began to consider the implications of the incarnation. While it remained problematic to depict God the Father, since no one had ever seen God and lived, because the Son had come to us as a human, the unknown had become known. God has a face and it is a face we have seen. Indeed, as Paul writes of Jesus, "He is the image of the invisible God, the firstborn of all creation."[50] Paul's word for image there, εἰκών, was not lost on advocates for the creation of icons. Paul appears to have knowingly given permission for claiming a certain knowledge of God, granted us only through the manifestation of Jesus, but granted so that we might access a more complete knowing of the One by whom all things were made. Too, the Holy Spirit became popularly depicted as a dove or as fire, as the third person of the Trinity had been made known in such forms in both the baptism of Jesus and at Pentecost. Debate continued in the church for hundreds of years about the appropriateness of making images of Jesus or of any holy person or event and this debate lives on, even today. Many Protestant traditions actively resist visual arts, for reasons either to do with perceived decadence or because of latent fears of idolatry. Such incredulity has robbed us at times of the good of iconography, a rich tradition of contemplating the holy in turn with offering artistic talent back to God.

A teacher in the early church, Saint Basil of Caesarea (c. 329–379), explained icons are akin to someone pointing to a statue of Caesar and, upon asking who it was, being told the statue was Caesar. Basil said we do not believe the statue to be literally Caesar or that there are two Caesars, but the statue is a location of our remembrance, such that what name, honor, or recognition it is given is passed on to the one to whom it refers. It grounds our focus. The gesture of honor shown toward the statue of Caesar is ultimately a gesture of honor shown toward Caesar himself. In the same way, the gesture of honor shown to a depiction of Jesus is a gesture of honor shown ultimately to Jesus himself. What's important about icons is how they are able to give our imaginations shape, guidance, structure. The earliest icons had specific rules governing their construction: colors, form, and text, all of which held deeply symbolic meaning. Icons were ways to visually explore the edges of our belief, the fields of orthodox Christian conviction and identity. The theological tradition that grew out of icons drew from the understanding that the creation was sacramental and advocated an approach to the world that affirmed partnership between God and humanity in creating new ways to discover God.

Traditional icons for the Western and Eastern churches followed similar restrictive patterns up until the thirteenth century. After the thirteenth century, iconography in the West granted more freedom to the artist while the East remains to this day specific in requirements for what can be called an icon. Traditionally, icons follow the strict form of being presented on flat panels or canvas with realistic depictions of the subject. Some common imagery guides the interpretation of the work, examples being Jesus having one small eye—emphasizing his humanity—and one large eye—emphasizing his divinity, or Mary holding a lily, a symbol of the annunciation, or Mary Magdalene holding an egg, a symbol of her witness to the resurrection. Interpretation of icons is inseparable from contemplation of icons. To interpret the eyes of Jesus as a reflection of his humanity and his divinity is to contemplate the humanity and divinity of Jesus. Recalling Basil's words about the statue, we can see how icons serve as places of remembrance. We remember the humanity and divinity of Jesus and, by doing so, we contemplate the humanity and divinity. Contemplation is a form of prayer in which we find ourselves awed, reverent, amazed once again by God. Icons are windows through which we look to be reminded of something about God we might otherwise forget. So too with Mary and the lily. When we contemplate the icon we are reminded of Mary's answer to the angel upon the announcement she would give birth to Jesus. "Be it unto me according to thy word," she entreats, and as we contemplate this response we pray for it to also be our own whenever God should come to us and ask us to do a work.[51] Further, with Mary Magdalene, we contemplate the mystery of witnessing the resurrection, our own aching desire to cling to Jesus and our commissioning to tell all people what and who we have seen.

Nontraditional icons involve similar elevations to contemplation but do not fall under the specific rubrics traditional icons require. I do not mean only abstract paintings of Jesus or statues of Mary holding the child Christ. I mean teacups and Advent wreaths and pinecones and corks from champagne bottles consumed years ago. If icons in a broad sense may be called locators of remembrance drawing us into contemplation about God, then even ordinary things, everyday things, may be known to us as icons.

Consider our discussion of the world as a sacramental place. Under such conviction we understand the whole of the creation to be in some way interconnected in its yearning for God. It follows that everything in this world is capable of being turned back to God, of turning our thoughts back to God. Saint Augustine (c. 354–430) speculates as much when writing about the gold of the Egyptians the Israelites took with them during the Exodus. Augustine grants the gold had been used to fashion idols, but he adamantly denies this to be the fault of the gold. There's nothing inherently bad about the metal, it's only the form it was given that needs redeeming. So, he replies, melt down the gold and make new things from it, things to serve God, things to keep our mind on God.[52]

I don't have a lot of golden idols lying around my house, but I have stemware that reminds me of Easter dinners when the curtains are thrown open and we shout, "Christ is risen!" Icons are the ordinary signs of miracle. There is never just a cup in this world when every cup brings to mind the cup held by Jesus on the night he was betrayed, when he said it held his blood shed for us. There is never just a bed when every bed brings to mind the command of God to speak of the stories of God at all times and in all places, in our lying down and our rising. There is never just a basin of water when all water is called holy because Jesus entered the waters of baptism with us, called himself living water at the well of Jacob.

While our dough is resting, we prepare the bowls in which it will undergo its final proof. This last bit of preparation helps us make round and sturdy bread. When choosing your bowls, if possible use bannetons, which are specially made baskets designed to accommodate particular weights of dough. For our purposes, two bannetons sized for 1.5 to 2 pounds of dough would be best, but if you're without a banneton—and most of us always are—a medium serving bowl will do in a pinch. (Bowls are icons too, if we will ourselves to see them as such. There is never just a bowl when bowls bring to mind the prayers of the saints being placed before God in heaven. There is never just a bowl when we think of them as open things waiting to be filled.)

The shape of the bowl is going to determine the shape of the dough, so you don't want something too large or you'll bake a very droopy flatbread by mistake. Once the dough is shaped, it will fill a banneton or bowl about halfway, which will leave enough room for the final rise.

To prepare the bannetons or bowls, spread out a piece of smooth linen for each. You can use a kitchen towel here, just not one that's got loose threads, because you'll end up baking them into the loaf. I use flour sack towels, which are cheap. Sprinkle a generous amount of flour on the towels and then line your bannetons or bowls with one each, floured side up. As a general rule, you want just enough flour so that the dough does not stick and little enough that your bread does not come out of the oven with big patches of burnt flour on it. There is a happy medium in just under ¼ of a cup, but even this is guesswork. That works in my kitchen with my towels and my bowls. You'll likely have to try a few times before you can say what measure is best for you. Once prepared, set the bowls aside while you wait for the bread to finish its rest from the previous shaping.

And take a moment to contemplate the bowls, prepared, waiting for bread to be placed within them. Are we prepared? Are we prepared for the Bread of Heaven to be placed within us? Are we open, expectant?

While the simple act of noticing is in one way exercising the discipline of remembrance, sometimes more guided focus is rewarding. When I have led people in this work in the past, I have tended to run across two dominant perspectives. On the one hand, people from Christian traditions that encourage artistic representation do not have difficulty contemplating traditional icons or modern interpretations of Jesus, Mary, the apostles, the saints, and others. On the other, people from Christian traditions that discourage artistic representation find this difficult. For them, the contemplation of icons often raises concerns they are giving in to a kind of idolatry. But for this, modern and contemporary art can be healing. Among the most prominent Christian artists in the tradition of nonliteral representation would be Makoto Fujimura, whose inspired paintings reflect Christian themes and biblical grounding but lack concrete depiction. For those who find difficulty with traditional icons or literal representation, Fujimura and other abstract artists may prove a soft-entry into the discipline of remembrance. This is because modern and contemporary art often lacks specific realism, which people who were raised to be uncomfortable with images in worship find challenging. The lack of realism invites the mind to wander beyond the fears of idolatry and to discover how God might engage them through the art.

In Appendix 2 on pages 171–72, you will find a list of suggested pictorial icons, traditional and nontraditional, which you may use to aid in the practice of contemplation. I approach contemplation through a fourfold practice similar to *lectio divina*, lasting about fifteen minutes. Once I've chosen an image to contemplate, I spend a few minutes getting quiet and still, remembering that since all things are able to participate in the work of God, the contemplation of this art is part of sacred work, an invitation to be formed more and more into the image and likeness of Jesus. Then, I begin:

1. *Observe.* Take in the piece as it is, without trying to read it too quickly. Let it strike you, the fullness of it, the space it takes up in your mind.

2. *Notice.* Let yourself focus in on a particular quality, perhaps that speaks of God or speaks of something in relation to God. Consider what you are noticing in relation to yourself. What about this feature speaks to you, to what end does it draw you?

3. *Converse.* Thank God or petition God, put that thing you have noticed in dialogue with who God is. Spend time here, listening and speaking with the Creator, offering praise for the blessing of beauty formed with human hands in partnership with the divine.

4. *Imitate.* Still yourself and evaluate how you can imitate the good quality of your Creator in response to what you have noticed. Then, as with *lectio* or the Examen, offer these things back to God and return to a place of stillness and peace.

My mother stands in the third kitchen I lived in, hands raised slightly as she recites a passage from Malachi. "But for you who revere my name, the sun of righteousness shall rise with healing in its wings. You shall go out leaping like calves from the stall."[53] It is the thirteenth year of her disease, a tangled malady of nerves and muscles, causing her to feel she is set on fire from head to toe unceasingly. It is the thirteenth year in which God has promised her healing in this life. It is the thirteenth year she has stood in our kitchen and recited the thirteen Scriptures of promise God gifted her as icons of hope. The Scriptures are framed, lining the sides and top of a window. Each has a story, each has a context of remembrance. The Scripture given at the moment of deepest despair, the Scripture given when the answer of healing was *not yet*, the Scripture given when one more step was needed on the path of trust. They have become timeless, these promises, framing the window in the kitchen. It's hard to say now where this story begins and ends. This world is full of healing that is both now and not yet. Here in this kitchen, where my mother professes the remembrance of promise once again, the work of those framed Scriptures, those icons, is most acute. Icons remind us of who we are and of who God is. The discipline of remembrance is what keeps us going on the days we would much rather turn back or sit down. The discipline of remembrance is what keeps us going on the days we would think ourselves sure enough to run ahead. Remembrance grants us enough meaning to occupy the here and now with as much insight as God would let us have. We don't know where this will take us, where this path is turning, but that it turns and winds us deeper into God.

"I recite them because they form me." My mother says this to someone visiting, while she pours tea. "They keep me mindful of what God has said, keep me mindful of what God has promised, and so when I say them I remind myself, find myself formed. It shapes me. Shapes how I think, how I believe. It's a way of keeping me honest. Really honest. Because I might think honesty is telling you how much pain I'm in, and I am, but that's not really honesty. Honesty would be telling you I am in so much pain but God has promised healing. Honesty would be telling you I have to cling to that promise every day and every hour. Honesty would be telling you some days all I have is reciting these Scripture and some days that's enough."

It is the thirteenth year of recitation. The thirteenth year of remembrance; yet it may as well be day one or year twenty-six. When she proclaims the promised truth, it is as fresh as the first hearing, as enduring if it takes decades. Still she returns to the icons, the promise kept in mind, and in the rootedness of their perspective, hope, where it would have died, thrives.

For the last shaping of our loaves, we work quickly and gently. Flour only your hands to avoid putting too much flour back into the dough. If it sticks to your counter, have your dough scraper ready to free it; again, avoid too much flour being incorporated. In the manner similar to what we have done before, turn the dough over so the seams face up once again and fold the dough as previously, working gently to not tear the surface of the dough. Cup your hands and roll the dough toward yourself, giving it a gentle quarter turn as you do so. Do this just a few times to put tension back in the shape, and then quickly deposit the blissful mass in your prepared proofing bowl, seams facing up. The top of the dough in the proofing bowl will become the bottom of the dough once it's baked, so don't worry too much about the look of it right now. Chances are, you're doing okay.

Gently cover the loaves with the overhanging towel and transfer them to the fridge. We do this for the final rise to slow the process of the yeast, which will give our bread excellent flavor. Over the next hour to an hour and a half, the dough will nearly double in size and take on the perfect round shape of the bowl it rests in. Near the end of the process, preheat your oven to 500F and, if using the preferred method with a Dutch oven as described in the recipe on pages 31–36, place it on the bottom rack of the oven to preheat as well. If your oven has a convection setting, do not use it. We are, at long last, ready to bake.

Everything has been prepared. Everything to do with shape and form has been done. Remembrance, the contemplation of icons, the noticing of the world, of the altars all around us, this work is about preparing us too. This work is about shaping us, slowly, with less forced effort and more room for the Spirit to come in, smooth our seams. Every place in this world can be a place where God is found. Every place in this world can be a place where God is finding us, preparing us, making us rise.

For This Week

DISCIPLINE

- Practice contemplation of an icon two times this week, each time for about fifteen to twenty minutes. As we discussed, you may use traditional icons or any sort of art that speaks to you. Engage all art critically, asking whether it speaks to you of the beauty of God or is not praiseworthy. Consider how the meditative engagement with remembrance and memory making shapes your day and your sense of place within it.

- Try your hand at making your own icon. Perhaps you draw or paint, abstract or concrete. See what comes out naturally and then spend some time reflecting on it. A good way to guide this work would be to read a passage of Scripture and then respond to it through artistry. I don't want to be too prescriptive on what making an icon would be for you. You know the edges of your creative self. Explore them.

- Take a few moments each day to consider the ordinary world around you and how it glimpses the past and the present and the future. Consider your relation to it, to others, and how awareness of connectivity, of the shared experience of all things, might lead you into deeper relationship with the world around you and with God.

BAKE

- Feel the limits of the dough this week, how it stretches and gives. This is the last time you'll put hands to the process before putting it in the oven, a triumph of a kind.

- Notice how temperature slows or speeds the process of the final proofing. Pay attention to the slightest changes as an opportunity to know how your dough feels about the environment you have put it in.

- Forgive yourself when you press too firm or split the surface or any other thing that can and will happen at this point. Breathe in deep, laugh a bit, try again.

ASK

- Where are the places in your life where the discipline of remembrance is ready to be found?

- Do you find yourself most comfortable with art that is concrete or abstract? Why?

- How does the discipline of remembrance shape your relationship to family or friends?

At the Table

In our last three weeks of study, we consider
disciplines focused on cultivating our relationship
to others in community.

  We will first explore how fasting keeps us mindful
of holy work, then how feasting is a necessary and vital
part of our lives, and then, finally, how seasons of life
ask of us different approaches in how we know God.

  Here is where we move toward an ending of a kind,
wanderers on this path without end. We look from
the world to those who have come to journey with us,
where God is meeting us along the way, where God is
urging us to keep on.

Baking: Fasting

◆───◆

Spring comes quietly to the path through the wood. Easter tends to be in April, if not very late March, which means for nearly a month of the secular season, when new life blossoms and makes itself known, you are walking in the spiritual season of Lent, of abstinence, and grieving the withering power of Death. When you aren't disposed to notice it, the contrast is subtle. You are aware there is incongruity with the rhythms of the church year and the rhythms of the world, but they are inconsequential. Except when creation is understood as an icon, because every defiant blade of grass and every bursting bud on tree limb pronounces God's making of all things new. You walk the season of want in the land of plenty.

Lent is the stretch of days in which we fast, keep a vigil of remorse for our sins personal and sins collective. It is a reminder that the tension we live in as Christians is the hope that there is better, even when it appears all has already been made whole. When we look beneath the new life, we find the death of life. When we turn the soil along the path, old roots and rotting form are to be found. It does not make the prophetic flower, declaring new life, straining toward the sun, any less significant or good, but it sobers us. In the spring you walk into the internal shadow of the valley of death and you know the interior darkness as well as you know the exterior sun.

We have spoken of patience often in relation to the work of making bread. The last step of patience is the oven, the passing of dough from hands into the fire to become whatever it shall be in the end. It's a different sort of patience in that way. Each period of waiting before this one had tangibility. Hands in dough learned if water was needed or another half hour on the warm windowsill. Hands in dough learned the rhythm of the yeast expanding and contracting, knowing when the shape was just set. But once the loaf is in the oven, it is beyond our grasp. No more fussing. This is akin to the want in the land of plenty. You can see the bread, but it is not yet yours to taste. This is akin to a fast. This week, we will explore the spiritual discipline of fasting while we contemplate the time of baking. We will examine the spiritual good of being mindful of death—all kinds of death—and what our want can teach us about who we are to God.

Like all disciplines, fasting can lean toward legalism rather quickly. One person fasts from all food for forty days because it is simply the custom to do so, while another gives up coffee for a week and tells everyone on Twitter about it. Both extremes are unhelpful. The scriptural accounts of fasting present us with diverse forms but unified motivation: seeking an answer from God. Fasting as repentance is seeking an answer from God that forgiveness has come; fasting as calling upon God for help and healing is a similar gesture of petition; likewise, fasting as discernment over a difficult decision or fasting as renewed focus upon God fundamentally are invitations for God to bring awareness, answer.

I want to stress this from the start of any discussion on fasting, because often fasting is presented as a rejection of the material world, a denial of the good of the physical creation. Fasting is not a gesture of protest, a condemnation of such good things like food and drink and television and the endless lists of things we name to give up. Fasting is a gesture of balance, giving up one thing to make room for another. When you fast from food for a day, when hunger comes harsh and demanding, you do not simply wait the hunger out. That's less a fast than it is mortification. A fast would be receiving the hunger and returning it as reminder in prayer. It may sound a bit silly, but there's something deeply known when you pray from your feeling of hunger to hunger for God in the same way. It is not that food is bad, but that the absence of food reminds us of its good, which in turn can remind us of the good of the God who provides all nourishment to our physical and spiritual being.

As Jesus instructs in Matthew 6,

> And when you fast, do not look gloomy like the hypocrites, for they disfigure their faces that their fasting may be seen by others. Truly, I say to you, they have received their reward. But when you fast, anoint your head and wash your face, that your fasting may not be seen by others but by your Father who is in secret. And your Father who sees in secret will reward you.[54]

Fasting is about connection to God, not about making a show of giving up. So when we speak of the discipline of fasting, we must also speak with great specificity about the posture of our hearts as we enter into it. Fasting is as much a sacrifice of praise as it is a denial of self, so when we approach the fast, it is a wise and prudent thing to examine our motives thoroughly. Whether we do so for a day, a week, a season—we do so because we long for God. The longing is the most important work of any fast. The longing is, like defiant blossoms in spring, both a sign of what is and a sign of what is to come.

We've been edging around the idea of sacramentality for a handful of weeks now. Discussing the Holy Spirit in our lives, recognizing how the world participates in the life of God along with us through the disciplines of wonder and remembrance. As we've come to understand, to speak of something as *sacramental* is to recognize all created things are connected to God by the fact of their creation. As a painting is never free from the vision and intention and direction of the one who painted it, so too this world and all of us are never fully free of God.

But because of the work of Jesus, we may go a step further. Jesus offered a way of having not only a sacramental understanding of the creation generally but also specific and particular means to encounter him: the sacraments. To build on language we have already been using, sacraments are icons. Sacraments, locations of our remembrance and windows through which to see the world anew, are also the means by which the power of God at work in us is refreshed. This phrasing can be a hindrance for people, because they are wary of what seems to be the spooky parts of Christianity. Sacraments are not magic, but they are not without power. Classically, sacraments are defined as "an outward sign of an inward grace," that is, what is seen and received externally is evidence of an interior work already in motion. Just as the invisible God becomes visible in the Incarnation, the sacraments make visible the invisible work of the Spirit within and around us. In the sacraments we say we meet Jesus particularly, specifically, because Jesus gave them to us for such purpose.

While there has been debate over the centuries about how many sacraments there are, an agreement across all liturgical traditions is to recognize two as fundamental: baptism and Communion, which is also called the Eucharist or the Lord's Supper. This is because Jesus specifically identifies these two events as places we encounter him.

Before ascending to heaven, the command Jesus gives to the men and women gathered on the mountain is for them to go and make disciples of all nations, which will be signified in their being baptized in the name of God, Father, Son, and Holy Spirit. Similarly, when Jesus gives the apostles Communion, he does so with the qualification they are to do it often, and as often as they do it, they are to do so in remembrance of him. The doing is remembrance making, icon making. Sacraments were gifted to us as tangible ways to encounter the intersections of the physical and the spiritual, the human and the divine.

How does a chapter on fasting relate to a conversation about sacraments? Death.

Death. Such a little word means all that.

We are sometimes a hasty people, skipping quickly to the end of the Gospels, to resurrection, to new life, to every good and perfect thing. Yet the path to that end is one that passes through the unwelcome country of loss and disconnection. There is no Easter without Good Friday, no glorified body without body bruised. Fasting is a reminder of our limits, of our desperate dependence upon God in all things, perhaps most particularly in relation to the impossible enemy of Death. For there is none other than God who can fight for us or stand against such a permanent end, none but God who can promise us safe passage through the country beyond this life.

Baptism is a sacrament rooted in death, though we often speak of it in terms of life. This is understandable, because we believe the confession of faith in Jesus Christ to be sufficient, to be the moment when the Holy Spirit like fresh fire on Pentecost descends and enters into the confessor. Yet when Paul writes about baptism, he lingers on the moment before, the sign of the sacrament itself:

> Do you not know that all of us who have been baptized into Christ Jesus were baptized into his death? We were buried therefore with him by baptism into death, in order that, just as Christ was raised from the dead by the glory of the Father, we too might walk in newness of life. For if we have been united with him in a death like his, we shall certainly be united with him in a resurrection like his.[55]

Burial proceeds resurrection, the fast comes before the feast. Both are expressions of trust and expected answer. I trust God will not leave me in the country of death but will answer by receiving me into God's presence. I trust God will not leave me in hunger but will answer by making a place for me at God's feast. The sacrament of baptism uniquely participates in pronouncing my being as hid in God, for in the waters I am lowered into the death of Jesus, identified fully and completely with Jesus in his death, so that in being brought up from them I may also share in his own rising again. Icons of remembrance are not mere memory. Remembrance is being brought into the fullness of existence offered to us, to be so much a co-heir with Jesus that we share in the very identity of Jesus ourselves. Our death is no longer our death alone, but our death is shared by and in Jesus so that we may share in his resurrection.

Paul identifies baptism as a sacrament by observing our passing into the waters as the visible sign of the invisible grace at work in us. We have been buried with Jesus, as Jesus, and raised to walk in life in the fullness of him. This is no magic, but it is no empty ritual. The waters are called holy and the work called efficacious, for it is here the unknown is proclaimed known, the soul in want is given its fill.

In turn, fasting, while not a sacrament, is a sacramental discipline. In fasting we encounter our dependence upon God anew. Fasting prompts us to long for God, to seek God, and to be less distracted by our comfort, which is often our greatest distraction. This too is something about death. Death makes us uncomfortable. It makes us consider what it is we call important, what it is we cede our time and energy to. Fasting, similarly, refocuses us on the essentials. Fasting keeps us mindful that what God has given us is not for us alone, but for all people, that if we grow too comfortable with what we have been given, we will be at its mercy when it is taken away.

I don't know if she ever roasted a chicken again after he died. He had hated garlic, so she always had to sneak it in below the skin, fishing it out before she served it, smeared with butter and rosemary. Rosemary, the herb of memory, now in proud unclipped stalks in the pot on the kitchen island where I slice apples to make a pie. It is seventeen days since my grandfather passed from this world into the next, just shy of fifty years married to my grandmother. I am making a pie to keep busy, in the aftermath of the funeral and visiting extended family. It's now just the small circle of us in a house that is too big, in rooms that echo nostalgia and stories so old and familiar they may very well be fiction. Death makes us all guilty of apocrypha, retelling the usual with new detail — he was wearing a red shirt, she had never driven to Memphis before — because detail becomes suddenly more important than the large fact of any one thing. Detail lets you hold on, lets you keep them in the room just a bit longer, with a name and a purpose and a knowingness unique to them and to you. This too will fade, but you have it for a little while more.

I put the pie into the oven and keep watch in the kitchen. I wash every dish I see, even ones already clean. I reorganize the pantry shelves, then put them back as they were originally. I am waiting for something, though I am unsure of what. An hour or so later, when the pie is resting on the wire rack and nearly cool enough to slice, my father comes into the kitchen and I know this is what I have been waiting for. I have been waiting for the fact of him, because it was his father lowered into earth and the visceral future of this turn between us became known in a way it had never been before. I had been waiting for him for the reassurance there was no apocrypha in my assessment of him, that he was and still was. I slice him a piece of pie, and we sit at the table, familiar but now other, one chair empty when it should not be, when it has never seemed to be before now, and we talk about the most ordinary of things because it will be this we miss the most and this he already misses.

We linger several hours, discuss the things that will need doing the next day, and then I say I'll clean the kitchen and he goes to find my mother. I wash the dishes with intense awareness, memorizing the ridges and dips of the plates, willing a certainty of this moment, that it would endure as long as I could keep hold of the feel of it. The pie is the last thing I put away, gently covered with a piece of plastic wrap, sealed like a tomb placed into the refrigerator, two small slices taken from it. It remained there, unspoken for, forgotten and yet remembered. A sign of something. A sign of something to come.

Since that night, I don't make apple pie very often.

If I had to choose only one thing I thought a kitchen required, it would be a Dutch or French oven.

The versatility of the pot is a wonder, transitioning from sauce making to poaching to baking with ease. I think it's such an essential, I feel confident saying you could get by in a kitchen if a Dutch oven was your only pot. I haven't tried this for myself, but experience would suggest it, given how much more often I reach for it than I do one of the other thirty-three pots lining our kitchen rack. Our Dutch oven is nothing extraordinary. While I will pledge all sorts of allegiance to the wonder and craft of Le Creuset, I am pleased to report our Dutch oven came to us from a big box store at about a sixth of the cost of the comparable model. Measuring in at just about 5.5 quarts and with a sleek enamel finish, the pot roasts a whole chicken or endures a half-day of soup making as well as any other I've used. Feel free to not shell out the several hundred dollars often assumed such a pot requires. There are fine, cheaper versions that not only do just as well but also are essentially indistinguishable from the more expensive models.

I stress all of this to emphasize my strong hope you will be using the Dutch oven method of baking bread and that if you have not, out of fear of expense, you need not be so inhibited. The Dutch oven method makes for the very best crust.

When your oven is preheated to 500F and the Dutch oven along with it, remove the Dutch oven and uncover it. Take one of the loaves of bread from the refrigerator and turn it over, seam-side down, into the Dutch oven. Using a very sharp knife cut a quick X in the surface of the dough, not too deep but with a long stroke to make a sizable X. Spritz the surface of the bread with water or gently apply the water with a pastry brush, cover it with the lid and return the whole back to the oven. Bake for fifteen minutes, then reduce the oven temperature to 450F and bake fifteen minutes more. Uncover the loaf and let bake another fifteen to twenty minutes until the crust is deep amber.

Remove the Dutch oven from the oven, and transfer your bread to a wire rack to cool. Allow the bread to rest for an hour before cutting into it to preserve the moisture. If you're following with the second loaf, return the Dutch oven to the oven, covered, and once again preheat to 500F, giving the Dutch oven ten minutes at this temperature before beginning again.

Dutch ovens are like caskets. It's too obvious a comparison not to make. The bread is placed into a heated tomb, sealed away, and something miraculous will come from it. But for a time it is hidden. For a time it is buried.

Lament is not something American Christianity tends to embrace, but we are in such need of it. Lament is audacious enough to recognize that though the Light is come, the darkness is not yet gone. Lament is confident enough in the work of the Light it does not shy away from admitting the destruction of the dark. Lament cries with the mother who holds the corpse of her child, does not assure her too quickly the child is now in a better place. Lament is unafraid of pain, agony, grief. Lament takes serious the sin in us and in this world, in the harsh and relentless truth that in this world there will be troubles.

Too often we don't want to admit there is suffering here and now, and such suffering is not abolished by claiming some abstract hope or attaching Jesus to every situation like he is a Band-Aid. The Great Physician does not heal with fairy dust or sleight of hand. The Great Physician comes into the place of the broken, sets limbs and bandages eyes, but does not deny the pain of the process, the grief of the loss, the strain of pushing through one more day. Fasting is one of the few disciplines that connects us to our physical bodies, to the frailty of being human, to the knowledge we are dying and surrounded by the dying and in the midst of dying and all of it can only be made right if Jesus wills it to be, but the willed is now and is not yet, this world is still in decay, this world will still pass away. There is in us a grief waiting to be named if we were only brave enough to name it.

There comes a point when the friends of Job say nothing, for they realize their words are worth nothing. The prophet Jeremiah is unashamed to remind Israel the great and deep darkness it walks through is because the world is a fragmented place of broken dreams. The manger is the only throne humans could give their Maker, but the Maker still comes and rests in it. The King of Glory flees forth from the House of Bread into the arms of poor sinners.

Fasting reminds us to grieve for the world in need. Fasting makes us uncomfortable enough to stop pretending Jesus is somewhere floating in heaven with a smile plastered on his face for all eternity.

Jesus is here in the emergency room of our being. Jesus is with us.

The discipline of fasting, when legalistically defined, loses so much of its good that I want to take care with it here. There are some guiding questions and principles of approach that are good to keep in mind as you proceed. One of the most important aspects of fasting is keeping silence about it, except when it is absolutely necessary to share it with others. Protecting yourself from the temptation to turn fasting into a performance is an easy enough thing to do by simply keeping your mouth shut. As to the *what* and *how* of a fast, this is the work of prayer. As we have considered, fasting isn't exclusively related to food, but food is often what people gravitate toward. Other fasts could be fasting from reading or social media, fasting from speaking, from driving. Fasts should be disruptive enough to the routine of life that you are aware of their inconvenience, which should press you toward refocusing your expectations and awareness of how much you depend upon God. Before you enter a fast, consider prayerfully exactly what you are to fast from and for how long. If you have never fasted before, it's a good idea to practice a shorter period of fast to get a feel for it and consider how it would affect you in a long-term engagement.

Particularly with any fast involving food or water, consult your doctor first. But if you wish to practice a fast from food, consider doing so based on a sundown-to-sundown model. Enjoy dinner as usual, then the following day skip breakfast and lunch and then eat dinner only after the sun goes down that day. This is usually a good place for those unused to fasting.

Remember too that fasting isn't only about giving up but taking on, so replace what time would have been spent eating a meal with prayer, Bible reading, volunteer work. If you are fasting from media, go for a walk when you would usually watch television, or call a friend who needs encouragement on your way into work instead of playing a podcast.

The fundamental part of a fast, beyond the act of giving up and taking on, is the prayerful consideration of sin in your life. Fasting is often linked to repentance, which connects it even more deeply to baptism. As you fast, in the same posture of consideration we took on with the Examen, ask the Spirit to reveal to you places in your heart you may have been ignoring or not considering fully. Don't be surprised if what turns up is a bit small, seemingly insignificant. Fasting can connect us to the deeper rhythms of the self and of God, to the places that seem insignificant but God would have us grow. Enter the fast with willingness to hear God in the smallest of things and, in turn, break your fast with a similar posture, grateful for what you have been shown, been granted to know.

What was hidden for a time, like bread in our oven, emerges well-formed, beautiful in its time, ready for the feast.

For This Week

DISCIPLINE

- Fast from something this week. Spend time in prayer as to what the thing should be, or perhaps the things, but observe your fast from Monday to Saturday then break it on Sunday, keeping the feast of the Lord. Consider what the dual action of giving up to take on taught you, what it brought forth in you, and whether you encountered God from a different perspective than you normally find yourself inhabiting.

- Consider your baptism. Spend some time during the week reflecting on its significance. Do you see in it a twinned response, a joy but a sorrow? In what ways? Record your thoughts, either in long form or as a list, and spend time talking to God about what you uncover as you explore your responses and convictions.

- Observe a day of silence. As much as possible, do not speak, read, watch TV, listen to music, or anything of the kind. Practice listening in the stillness and meeting God in the place of removal.

BAKE

- Observe your bread after you uncover it while it bakes. Notice it. Consider it. Watch the ways it rises and firms and takes shape under the heat.

- Be aware of your senses while you wait for the bread to finish. Smell the delicate change of flour and yeast, feel the warmth that occupies the space like a halo around the oven door. Take notice of your body in a similar way as when you practiced wonder. Waiting, absence, fasting can teach us much about the power of physical presence.

- Notice the texture of the bread while you let it cool, how the crust feels when you press against it a half hour after, an hour after it's out of the oven. This gives you a sense of how bread settles as it cools.

ASK

- If you came from a Christian tradition that encouraged fasting, did it also encourage the replacing of the fasted from thing with a kind of devotion, giving up to take on? If not, how did that shape your understanding of fasting?

- The seasons of the church year provide particular times in which we fast collectively, not individually. What do you think is the advantage of observing a fast together as opposed to alone?

- For many, fasting is a hard discipline because it is too often presented as hatred of the body or the physical world. After thinking about fasting this week, do you find fasting to be a hatred of the body? Why?

Serving: Feasting

E ventually, the path ends. Or, if it doesn't exactly end, you arrive. From my apartment and through the woods you find yourself in town. St. Andrews is a sleepy university village of no more than three major streets. The path quits on one edge of the town gate, but if you press on you find yourself still tracing it behind gardens and shops until you reach the far gate of St. Mary's, the divinity school with its large and fearsome tree in the courtyard allegedly planted by Queen Elizabeth II, though she really planted the small tree in the corner that has become so frail it needs a rod beneath its branch to support it.

The tree with its support is as essential to the path as the shape of it upon the earth. Humans were created for community. The myth of our coming into being suggests that as varied and wondrous all living things are, it is only a fellow human that satisfies deep and pressing needs within us. Community is the blessing of the path, the discovery that we both do not walk it alone and there are people waiting for us on the other side. The layers of the gift are infinite — there is a great feast toward which we all journey, toward the place where Jesus says he will eat of the bread and drink of the cup with us again, but there are the lesser feasts leading up to the last, the places where in small ways we gather and mark the bounty of the creation and the good of its offerings. Feasting is a practice essential to the Christian experience because we are a people for whom feasting makes the most sense. We are redeemed, our God has walked into the midst of Death and abolished it. It has been said of us that "the people who walked in darkness have seen a great light; those who dwelt in a land of deep darkness, on them has light shone."[56] If we fast, we must feast, for in the places we acknowledge death and sin we also declare life and redemption. Jesus has come into the midst of us, and all is being made anew. Feasting is an act of defiance against the powers of evil in the cosmos, a declaration the battle has already been won, God has already declared victory.

Eating the bread you have made might seem the easiest task of all the parts of baking we have explored, but it can sometimes prove the least rewarding. When we forget to savor, to taste the goodness of the thing, we put our effort to shame. Sometimes we need to remind ourselves to go slow, to truly taste, to learn the bittersweet of yeast and the salty burn of crust. The reward of a good bread, its flavor and texture and shape, is a common miracle, deep and ancient power made known in the most ordinary of circumstances. In a week where the discipline is to feast and the encouragement is to eat, let me stress first and foremost a feast is made up of everyday things like bread, but it is the posture of heart, as with fasting, that makes a feast a feast. Central to a feast is the table, the place where we come and share with one another, where we exchange our own discoveries made along the path, learn and collaborate and marvel. The table around which we feast is an icon of remembrance, a vision of the great ultimate table God has prepared for us. At this table all of us are equal, all of us are given our fill. At this table, it doesn't matter if you have been here for years or have just found the path's end, there is a place for the old and the young, food enough for the famished and the peckish, before the journey begins again, the path returned to.

This week we consider the discipline of feasting, perhaps one of the most deceptively easy endeavors we take on as followers of the risen Jesus. As we do, we will keep in mind what it means that there is always an end to a feast in this life, how until the end of all things we will not fully share the great feast of our Lord together—how this is our directive to push out onto the path again, and again, and again.

In the Eucharist, Jesus makes himself known to us in a unique and profound way. I make some assumptions here, which need establishing. First, Communion is a significant part of the life of the church and is ideally received as often as possible. This comes from the Scripture. As Luke tells of the earliest days of the church in Acts, "And they devoted themselves to the apostles' teaching and the fellowship, to the breaking of bread and the prayers."[57] Historically, the church has recognized the breaking of the bread described by Luke to not only include all sorts of shared meals together but also to indicate a culminating feast shared around the table of the Lord in the Eucharist. It wasn't until the Reformation and the multifaceted splintering of denominations that followed that Communion was increasingly resisted for fear of it being abused, misunderstood, or seeming too Roman Catholic.

But if Communion is important, then history aside, Jesus is the one who will tell us why.

The gospel of John is not considered a synoptic gospel, as it does not follow a historical timeline of the life of Jesus. John focuses on signs and symbols, ordering narratives to reveal deep theological truths. Events are often situated in such a way to provide comment, contrast, compliment, or metaphorical import to one another. When we look at John 6, for instance, a passage that will culminate with Jesus saying some very hard things to hear about his flesh and his blood, we notice how the progression of events begins with the feeding of the five thousand. A passage that will end with Jesus calling himself the bread of life opens with Jesus literally feeding thousands of people with bread that he has blessed to be multiplied. Further, it is shortly thereafter we read about Jesus walking on the water, a miracle directly speaking to two events at once. The first is creation. "The earth was without form and void, and darkness was over the face of the deep. And the Spirit of God was hovering over the face of the waters."[58] Since we know that it is through Jesus all things were made, this image is a repetition of the oldest of God we have — God on the water, calling forth life.[59] Second, in a passage where John is about to share with us Jesus's teaching on Communion, the disciple introduces the conversation by not so subtly referencing a baptismal image beforehand. In baptism we are called a new creation, made so by Jesus, through whom the old creation came into being. This link was surely not lost on the inspired writer of the gospel, and it is a sobering scene leading into what Jesus then teaches.

The crowd presses in close to the rabbi, and to them Jesus says, "I am the bread of life; whoever comes to me shall not hunger, and whoever believes in me shall never thirst."[60] Jesus goes on to say whoever believes this has eternal life, but the crowd is dissatisfied with the response. They press him for clarity, suppose him to be mad, to which Jesus answers more defiantly:

> "I am the bread of life. Your fathers ate the manna in the wilderness, and they died. This is the bread that comes down from heaven, so that one may eat of it and not die. I am the living bread that came down from heaven. If anyone eats of this bread, he will live forever. And the bread that I will give for the life of the world is my flesh."[61]

Pause a moment. Don't let yourself explain that away too quickly, don't look for an answer that is too comfortable, too convenient. These are hard words, difficult words, and we should not be surprised the crowd who heard them scoffed, demanding to know how Jesus would give them his flesh to eat.

> So Jesus said to them, "Truly, truly, I say to you, unless you eat the flesh of the Son of Man and drink his blood, you have no life in you. Whoever feeds on my flesh and drinks my blood has eternal life, and I will raise him up on the last day. For my flesh is true food, and my blood is true drink. Whoever feeds on my flesh and drinks my blood abides in me, and I in him. As the living Father sent me, and I live because of the Father, so whoever feeds on me, he also will live because of me. This is the bread that came down from heaven, not like the bread the fathers ate, and died. Whoever feeds on this bread will live forever."[62]

People have tried to soften the gravity of these words. They have supposed them to speak only to spiritual things, abstract and without physicality. Such interpretations conveniently ignore how if we believe all the gospels to proclaim truth, then Matthew, Mark, and Luke agree it is at the Last Supper Jesus illumines the meaning of his words. Jesus says unless we eat of his flesh and drink of his blood, we will not have life in us. At the Last Supper, Jesus takes bread, takes wine, says these are his body and his blood. We cannot overlook the connection, we cannot deny its presence. A difficult line, to be sure. The Scripture tells us many stopped following Jesus after he said these things. But when Jesus asks the disciples if they too would leave, Peter replies, "Lord, to whom shall we go? You have the words of eternal life, and we have believed, and have come to know, that you are the Holy One of God."[63] This is perhaps what Paul means in his letter to the Corinthians about discerning the body: they are to encounter Jesus in Communion in such a way as to recognize, to come to know, that he is the Holy One of God.

What is the Eucharist? What does it do?

These questions are good ones but, as we have seen, difficult ones. To begin with, in considering John 6, it occurs to me that the passage in which Jesus speaks of eating his flesh and blood is preceded by his walking on water, which we have noted is a connection to both the creation of the world and the new creation we are given in baptism. But to think of baptism is to think of Jesus's baptism, that the baptism of Jesus marks the first time in Scripture God enters the waters of the creation. In Genesis the Spirit of God hovers over them, in Exodus God parts the sea and makes dry land before moving on. It is only in the baptism of Jesus the waters are not cast away but indwelled. Would it be such a stretch to suggest that in the same way God was willing to become fully human, in the same way God enters into the waters, God mystically enters ordinary bread and ordinary wine? — bread and wine like water in baptism made holy simply by the action of the sacrament itself, are made for us the place where we encounter the life-giving Jesus in a unique and particular way. In a broad sense, this is often called Real Presence, the belief that Jesus is mystically made known to us through the bread and the wine. It is not mere symbol and certainly not mere memory, but a place of remembrance, icon, sacrament, a place where our unity to Jesus and to each other in Jesus is pronounced and strengthened and confirmed.

Traditionally, we say Communion empowers us to do the good we have been given to do. Jesus says it is his flesh and his blood that keep us in eternal life, that sustain us, and so when we encounter Jesus in the bread and the wine, when Jesus is made known to us in that particular way, it is a moment in which we are being directly fed by Jesus from his table. If we hold to wonder, to rootedness, to remembrance, we know that when we share in the meal at that table we do so not alone but with the disciples who first received it, with all those faithful gone before us, with all those faithful yet to come. Communion is the event in which we are connected within and outside of time to Jesus and to one another, for we all share in this meal together, we all are empowered for the kingdom work together. What the Eucharist does in us is feed us to, in turn, go out into the world and feed it. To offer what we have been given to those yet to receive it, to bring them back with us to the table to encounter Jesus for themselves, to eat of his flesh and drink of his blood, to know what it means to be a temple of the Holy Spirit, indwelled by the very God who made them.

Though there are so many places to look in the Scriptures when it comes to feasting, I am drawn to Luke's account of the disciples on the road to Emmaus. In the early days of the resurrection of Jesus, while he is ministering in various places before his ascension, Luke tells us there are two disciples walking toward Emmaus, dismayed by the death of the Lord. They had not heard he had been resurrected, and when Jesus joins them on their journey, they do not recognize him at first. Jesus asks why they are troubled, and they explain, to which he offers a gentle rebuke before beginning to reveal, using the Old Testament, how all things were foretold and necessary for the work of God's redeeming the world. The disciples are amazed by these insights and ask Jesus, whom they still do not recognize, to share a meal with them.

> When [Jesus] was at table with them, he took the bread and blessed and broke it and gave it to them. And their eyes were opened, and they recognized him. And he vanished from their sight. They said

to each other, "Did not our hearts burn within us while he talked to us on the road, while he opened to us the Scriptures?" And they rose that same hour and returned to Jerusalem. And they found the eleven and those who were with them gathered together [and] they told what had happened on the road, and how he was known to them in the breaking of the bread.[64]

Notice. The disciples only recognize Jesus once the bread is broken, a gesture mimicking the Last Supper. If we believe this is an event not isolated to this one time, but an icon, we may believe we also encounter Jesus, recognize Jesus, in the breaking of the bread. This conclusion is bolstered by Luke's word choice. When Luke says Jesus broke the bread, the word he uses to describe the action makes only two appearances in the New Testament, both of which are used by Luke. The first is here, in reference to Jesus breaking the bread at the table; the second is when Luke is describing the earliest days of the church, when he says the gathered people devoted themselves to the apostles' teaching, to the prayers, and to the breaking of the bread.

We do well to not try and overly define anything concerning the Eucharist. What I believe the Scripture presents us with is this: Jesus is recognized in the breaking of the bread in Communion and that Communion is significant enough that the early church observed it as regularly as they observed meeting together to learn, pray, and evangelize their communities. It is significant enough that Paul reminds the Corinthians of its specific instructions and urges them to take it seriously, reverently, or risk punishment. As the apostle warns, "Whoever eats the bread or drinks the cup of the Lord in an unworthy manner, shall be guilty of the body and the blood of the Lord ... that is why many of you are weak and ill, and some have died."[65]

What does it mean to receive Communion in an unworthy manner? Communion demands a reverence in us we are not always wanting to give. While I could spend a good deal of time just writing about that, I am hesitant to do so. I am hesitant because I am aware I'll risk speaking more of my preference than what I could justify by

Scripture, so in this I must leave a good deal of work to you and the Spirit. What does the Spirit tell you it means to receive Communion well, to discern the body, to not shame the person of Jesus as Jesus is made known to you in the breaking of the bread?

What is the discipline of feasting and what does it have to do with Communion? You would think no one needs to be instructed to feast, but too often the church does not encourage celebration in proportion to the encouragement of abstention. We hear how we should mortify the body, deny ourselves pleasure, but rarely how we have cause to eat good food, drink good wine, bake cakes, and order another round of oysters. The Communion meal is a feast, the place where Jesus meets with us in a specific way, and if we may say the table is a place of remembrance, icon, then no table is ever just a table once the table is called the place where Jesus comes to be recognized by us in the breaking of the bread. That is not to say every meal *is* the Eucharist or every table *the* place where Jesus is present in bread and wine, but it is to radically affirm the words of Jesus when he says, "For where two or three are gathered in my name, there am I among them."[66] When we come together around a table, when we come together professing the name of Jesus, Jesus tells us he is present with us.

As temples of the Holy Spirit, we are being ever-refined into his likeness, which is perhaps most apparent when we recognize the likeness of Jesus in one another as we metaphorically or literally break bread. It is said often that life is done around the table, but it is too often underappreciated how deep this work runs in us. It is not merely that when we are around a table we are sharing stories, encouraging one another, or seeking forgiveness. What we are doing is an icon of what is happening at the great table, the feast table of Jesus. We are mirroring the connectedness of the life of God and, as we mirror, participating in it. If the world is a sacramental place, if all things are connected to the One from whom they have their being, then each time we encounter one another we are participating in a small way in the great, large symphony of creation that finds its agency, life, and being in and through God.

Our tables point us back to the Table. Our guests point us back to the Guest.

Feasting is a discipline of trust, of declaration to the world that there is a God who has made all things and is making all things new through the power of the Spirit at work in and around us to fashion us all into the full image and likeness of Jesus Christ. Feasting is a protest against Death, for the Jesus who died has risen indeed, not only risen but is resurrected, and so there is cause to rejoice, to celebrate, to spend the fifty days of Easter popping champagne. In measure with our great need for lament we are also in great need of joy. Joy that does not diminish the real hurt of this world, that does not bid the grieving be silent, but joy that points back to the table where in the breaking of the bread Jesus is recognized, joy that causes us to say to all whom we meet, in the words of the Samaritan woman, "Come and see a man who told me everything I ever did! Could he possibly be the Messiah?"[67]

Though there are many, many delicious ways to make use of fresh bread, perhaps none are as satisfactory as slathering it with butter and preserves. For the initiated baker, unsalted butter reigns supreme for all usual baking needs. Unsalted butter ensures we don't add more salt to a recipe than is called for; salt also masks odors and flavors while preserving the butter, which means it's possible to be using less than fresh butter in a recipe and not know it until the end result isn't quite as good as we hoped for. I grant an exception in my kitchen, which is the good of salted butter on bread. While unsalted wins my affections every time, followed with a sprinkle of salt when needed, when it comes to fresh bread there's something different about butter already salted and generously leveled across the porous surface that is unparalleled.

As for the preserves, store-bought is just fine. Especially when the bread comes out in late evening, there's satisfaction in being able to quickly laden a slice with sweet and gooey fruit, a dessert unmatched when it's just past midnight. But sometimes you have enough guile and you want to do the work of making your own, an effort that will reward you handsomely. When the mood strikes me, I turn to strawberries. To make a very simple strawberry preserve, put a pint of trimmed and quartered strawberries in a saucepan with 1½ cups sugar, 4 tablespoons balsamic vinegar, 2½ tablespoons water, and 1 teaspoon of fresh cracked pepper. Bring the mixture to a boil, skimming the foam from time to time to remove any debris. Simmer, stirring occasionally and skimming as well for about fifteen minutes until thickened and the syrupy mixture is translucent. Cool completely before transferring to an airtight container and putting into the fridge. The preserves will last like this for about a month or, realistically in my house, about three days.

Alternatively, consider making a sweet butter if you've had enough of the salt. To do so, simply take a stick of room-temperature unsalted butter and ¼ cup good quality honey and whip them together using a stand-mixer for five minutes, until creamy and smooth. To this add ½ teaspoon each of vanilla extract and cinnamon, followed by 3 tablespoons toasted coconut. Whip for another two minutes. Store in an airtight container in the fridge for up to two weeks or shape into a log before storing. Again, you'll be making more of this soon. I'll warn you now.

I didn't go to church on Easter Sunday. In the year of the impromptu Maundy Thursday Communion around my kitchen table, I didn't make the walk along the path to the church in town. There was no specific reason for this, maybe a hundred or so small ones. It is a year of sadness, of disconnect. I don't know at the time this place is not where I am supposed to stay, but I am making every effort to convince myself it is.

But they have come now, a good twenty of them, filling the apartment with shoes and coats and side dishes. There are loaves of bread on the table, risen high, and a ham coming out of the oven. There's the usual frenzy, trying to figure out where everyone will fit. They have all been to church, some at dawn and some only just. There is a bourbon punch being cooled on the floor by the balcony, which even lukewarm begins to flow freely. There is laughter and reminiscence and shouts of "Christ is risen!"

They stay for hours, talk long of Easters past. A few remain to clean, even though I beg them to go. Cleaning helps me come back to myself, to focus. I am washing dishes and scrubbing the floor, finding God in the motions as I remember sadness and weariness and deep longing are not answered in solitude. I have been gifted in this company of guests with the reminder that the risen Jesus comes to us. Jesus comes into the midst of us and calls us by name. The Good Shepherd knows my name, and my friends are reminders, celebrants of the risen Jesus, that he still knows my name even when the season turns to weariness when it is time to feast.

So I bundle my coat, find my shoes, and make the walk that evening into town, along the endless path, to the church at the end. I walk up to the Table of God and meet again the Jesus who will welcome all who would come. Sometimes feasts help us the most. Sometimes what you need is not someone to sit with you in your pain as much as you need someone to remind you how to still feast.

In Communion we are all equal, for it is at this table princes and midwives and shepherds and CEOs and students and cabaret singers and librarians all come to encounter Jesus. Jesus does not withhold himself from anyone but offers freely to all who would receive. His table is open, welcome, ready. So if we speak of a discipline of feasting, it is along such lines we must model our own work. This will look different for you than for me, so the Spirit is essential to the discernment of how and in what way feasting should be made habit in your own life. But consider these questions as you seek God: the question of purpose and the question of guest.

The question of purpose when it comes to feasting can be a tricky one. We are used to coming up with reasons to fast, but reasons to feast often seem beyond our reach. Perhaps the simplest reason is the most obvious, that if we believe God desires intimate relationship with us, that if God has pronounced the creation, though fallen, to still be good and holy, then that is cause enough to throw a party. So celebrate the common things, the good grade or the successfully baked bread or the on-sale rack of lamb. Celebrate the things that God has called good, that God has shown care for, that God sees as remarkable while we tend to see ordinary. For around the table Jesus meets us, for around the table we meet Jesus in each other.

The question of guest when it comes to feasting is a bit easier. You cannot feast alone in a similar way that you cannot receive Communion alone. As the Eucharist is a sacrament that not only serves as sign to our unity with Jesus but also to one another in the mystical body of Christ, our feast table is no feast without others to share it with, to keep the feast with. So you pick up the phone and call some friends and have them 'round, because that is the comfortable thing. But there is the tension. If we have seen anything in the course of these chapters, surely it is Jesus is not content with our comfort. I heard Michel Martin in an interview once describe her ethos when approaching religious journalism as looking for who is not at the table and inviting them. Simple as that. She looked around to see who wasn't at the table and then made that person an invitation. I think that's the best guideline for a discipline of feasting: look around at your table and see who is not there — the neighbor next door, your butcher, a colleague at work — and make them a welcome guest. Offer the best place at the table. Gift the best you have on hand. For if the table we encircle is icon of the table of our Lord, then it is the place where Jesus gives the best to every person, regardless of how long they have been there, how they arrived there, where they sit.

It is only when we are at peace in ourselves, enchanted with the creation, and in desperate love with God we are able to make room at the table for another to come and meet God as we have, to learn how they have met God, to share in the great mystery of the God who has come near to us, is in us, is making us new. Again and again and again.

For This Week

DISCIPLINE

- Plan a feast. Remember a feast is not based on what is served but the spirit in which it is served. But to that end, make everything intentional, special, marked with significance. This week is a culmination of all we have considered previously, about the good of the physical world and its gift to us.

- Seek ways to include new faces, voices, and perspectives at your table or brave the step of seeking a place at theirs. In the former, make generous room to allow others to be treated with reverence, in the latter, make generous room in yourself to speak little, listen much, wonder and ask and learn.

- Mark an ordinary day with extraordinary thanksgiving, choose the most ridiculous but good thing to celebrate and celebrate it well. Live into the invitation to delight in the generosity of God and encourage your family and friends to do the same.

BAKE

- Make a bit of preserves or sweet butter as described on pages 145–46 and savor the sweetness of it smeared on fresh bread.

- Notice the final product of your bread, how it held up and settled out, if it's a bit dry or a bit damp, if it's just right or lacking. Compare it to previous attempts and consider what factors may have been involved in producing a different effect.

- Give your second loaf away to a neighbor this week, seek to make a friendship or bridge of community where there was not one before.

ASK

- Have you considered seemingly ordinary things in your life as worthy of feast? Why or why not?

- Some come from traditions accustomed to fasting, to legalism, to regimen, but rarely extravagance or celebration. Why do you think that is?

- What might be some ways the discipline of feasting and celebration can become more pronounced in your life as intentional, not just happenstance?

Setting to Rights:
Seasons

⟫⟫⟫—⟪⟪⟪

We've returned to the path. Perhaps we've returned to the beginning.

There are points on the path it seems unclear as to whether or not it will end.

You have passed the same row of houses twice now, haven't you? The budding yellow flower proudly pushing through the fencepost was noticed before, though was that today or yesterday?

This is where the metaphor becomes weak.

The literal path through that wood in Scotland had a definitive beginning and end—my apartment, the edge of town. The figurative path does not have such specific markers. Perhaps we could say birth and death and then something akin to living but only more so. Or, if inclined, baptism and then last rites and then, again, something akin to life but more than life alone: life abundant.[68]

The path of spirituality, of entering further and further into the life of God to which we have been invited, is less like a line and more like a circle. Perhaps not even a circle, but a Möbius strip. A Möbius strip is formed when an otherwise ordinary strip of paper is twisted and then bent back on itself to make a loop. The result is no matter where you start on the strip, if you draw a straight line and keep going, you will eventually come right back to where you began, having traversed the entirety of the strip inside and out without lifting your pencil or reaching an endpoint. You have journeyed the entirety of the path and yet you are back to where you started.

I think Christianity is a both/and in this way.

There is something to be said about the path of life that leads us forward into the future, into the next and the hereafter, but there is something also to be said about spiritual formation as a continuum. Patience when you are wrangling a toddler is different from patience when you are saving to purchase your first house, but not entirely so. You look around at your interior life and find the familiar things: anxiety, frustration, exhaustion, and though you learned the work of patience before, you seem to be learning it again, slightly different, slightly the same. So in summer you think you have learned something of intercessory prayer, but in winter it seems harder and less familiar than before. In spring you practice *lectio divina* and find the Scripture blossom within you only to come into autumn dejected and bored.

The path is not without seasons, without the length of time you cannot take the low bridge because of the summer floods or the period when the upper ridge is slick with ice in winter and untenable to cross. The path bids you turn one way, explore a new place, return somewhere forgotten until now. The path does not insist on one way forward, but that the going is forward enough, the keeping on enough to lead toward the end. The path assumes and perhaps even delights in differences of approach. I imagine God is equally so pleased.

This week, our last week, we consider the discipline of seasons and cleaning up the kitchen after a day of baking, of what it means to take stock of ourselves and the journey behind and ahead as the path of our lives winds on.

Perhaps the least glamorous of all things related to baking is cleaning your oven. A clean oven ensures temperatures stay within the ranges we need them to, our bread does not take on strange greasy flavors of pizzas cooked years before, and ensures the longevity of the faithful friend of the baker. Generally speaking, an oven doesn't need cleaning but every six months. If there's a spill, grease buildup, or other obvious dirtiness than you may need to do it sooner, but I have found most of the time a steady routine every half-year to be adequate. (In fact, I time the cleaning of our oven with the church year. I clean in the first week of Advent and in the first week after Pentecost. It's a few days shy of a perfect 180, but it's easy to remember.) Some ovens are self-cleaning, a feature often charming in the first years of use but unreliable as time goes on. I've found in years four or five the self-cleaning process sets off smoke detectors and, horrifically, sometimes sets grease and buildup even more firmly on the oven's interior. I don't think there's one thing holy about making more work for yourself than you need to, so I firmly suggest avoiding the self-cleaning lure unless you have certainty of its efficaciousness.

For the rest of us who remain skeptics, the work is not all that cumbersome. Obtain a bottle of white vinegar and a bit of baking soda and you're already on your way. Add to this repertoire an old towel and a bit of dish soap—natural, free and clear is just fine and, in my opinion, ideal—and really you're down to just some finagling and waiting.

To clean your oven:

1. Remove everything from the oven, including thermometers or pizza stones or anything of the like. Remove the racks of the oven, and, per advice from the excellent food blog, *The Kitchn*, put an old towel on the bottom of your bathtub and place the racks atop it. The towel will keep the racks from scratching your tub.

2. Clean the oven racks by filling the tub with hot water until the racks are just covered and add ½ cup natural dish soap to the water. Leave to soak for six hours or overnight, then use a sponge to buff away any grime on the racks. Give them a good rinse, a thorough drying, and they should be ready to go.

3. While the oven racks soak, turn your attention to the oven itself. Make a spreadable paste of baking soda and water, usually about ½ cup baking soda to just over 3 tablespoons of water should do nicely. Put on some rubber gloves, and then coat the entire interior of your oven with the paste, avoiding the heating elements. The paste will turn brownish in some places, especially as it meets grease or grime, and may also turn chunkier in some spots. That's no problem. Keep at it. Get everything covered,

again, avoiding the heating elements, then close the oven and let it sit overnight.

4. Take a damp cloth and wipe out your oven, picking up as much of the paste as you are able to. It may flake a bit or smear, just give the whole thing a good scrub. Some paste might resist you, which is no problem. Remedy this by spraying—or, in my case, flicking—a bit of white vinegar on any remaining baking-soda paste, which will foam nicely. Wipe down the oven again, adding more water or vinegar to the cloth to help shine the surface of the oven and to get rid of any remaining baking-soda paste.

5. Replace everything you originally took out of the oven, along with the now-cleaned racks, and you're all set.

From the beginning of this book we have spoken about the seasonal quality of faith. Faith is not something easily mapped, something we can say will always be and appear in this way or that. The cultivation of different disciplines of prayer and engagement with the world and God's presence within it allows us to anticipate the shifts and changes within our hearts, supplying us with new ways of encountering the divine when old ways turn stale. When we consider the partnership of the Holy Spirit within us, bringing us ever into a fuller, more truthful representation of the likeness of Jesus, we do so with knowledge that partnership obligates our participation. We practice spiritual disciplines as a way to deepen our work with the Spirit, to habituate in ourselves the desire to be as Jesus and as Jesus would have us be.

Sometimes we get discouraged, however, when it seems that we are doing all the things we should be but God seems far off, far from us, that the word begun within us in the power of the Spirit will go unfinished. It is in these moments the disciplines seem to betray us, unfulfilling in their promise to keep us rooted to God. While we may remind ourselves that wonder teaches us to look for God in all things, that remembrance teaches us to encounter God in the myriad icons in this world, it sometimes is a poor medicine.

This is when we must lean hardest on the Spirit and on each other. In the seasons of discontent, God has gifted so many ways in which we might encounter God. Take up one of the other disciplines, try it out for a while. Go to your friends, your family, and seek out the ways in which God may speak to you through them. There are seasons in life when the bread burns, when it goes stale. There are seasons when we think we cannot pray one more prayer or practice one more turn of the Examen. There is room for even this on the path of a life hid in God. You are a temple of the Holy Spirit, empowered by God to make God's name known in this world, but there's no one way to do that, no only way to do that, except that it is only by and through Jesus Christ. On this foundation everything is built, so when the season of the storm, the hail, the fire sets in, do not fear. You are not abandoned, God is not removed. As Jesus assured us, "All that the Father gives me will come to me, and whoever comes to me I will never cast out."[69]

In these moments, consider the diversity of the disciplines we have practiced, if perhaps it's time to put down one and take up another, if Jesus is perhaps leading you to consider a different way of encountering him or showing him to the world around you. In the moment of uncertainty, pause, breathe, look around. Where is God to be found in this place and time?

Ask this often, ask this daily, and wherever you see a glimmer of truth, of hope, of Jesus, walk that way. Trust that the One who formed you will not abandon you, that the One who guides you does not guide you unsafely. God may not be a God of our comfort, but God is a God of our good.

Sometimes the bread will burn. I can give ample testimony to it. Never fear, because this too does not go wasted. Oftentimes the burnt bits can be cut off and what lies beneath, though not exactly presentable, is nonetheless delicious. Many things in this life can be healed with butter and preserves. If the bread is so far gone, however, that even such means of common magic are of no help, there is still hope. Slice up any burnt bread and put it back in a hot oven to burn it just a bit more, until burned evenly. Allow the bread to cool until easily handled with your bare hands and crumble it into a fine, ashen texture. You now have a very simple fertilizer, which you can use on its own, sprinkled in your garden or outdoor potted plants, or add it to your compost pile. The same can be done with stale bread, of course, though I consider stale bread to be more readily salvageable in particularly delicious ways.

Stale bread makes for excellent croutons. Tear it into bite-size chunks, and for every cup of bread chunks toss them in about four tablespoons of olive oil—more or less—and give them a dash of salt and pepper, along with crushed garlic and chopped parsley if you insist on being generous, and put the lot spread out on a baking sheet in a 350F oven for about thirty to forty minutes until golden brown, stirring the croutons every ten minutes to brown evenly.

Alternatively, and preferably, stale bread makes excellent bread pudding, for which recipes abound online, but in our kitchen we tend to observe the simple approach of a greased 13" x 9" x 2" pan and an oven preheated to 350F. To about 3 cups of stale bread chunks (or cubes, if uniformity appeals to you) scattered in the greased pan, pour over a mixture of well-whisked together 2 cups white sugar, 5 large eggs, 1 cup whole milk, 1 cup half-and-half, 1 tablespoon vanilla extract, and ¼ cup of good bourbon, and let the bread soak this generosity up for at least ten minutes. In another bowl, mash ¼ cup soft unsalted butter with ½ cup dark brown sugar, 1 cup chopped pecans, and 1 tablespoon cinnamon, which you sprinkle over the soaked bread before putting it in the oven to bake for about thirty-five to forty-five minutes, until the bread pudding is set. Remove from the oven to cool while you make a hasty sauce in a small saucepan of 1 cup white sugar, ½ cup melted unsalted butter, and 1 beaten egg whisked over medium heat until the sugar is melted, to which you add ¼ cup bourbon or calvados, give a quick mix, and pour over the warm bread pudding before serving.

I suppose you could also use stale bread as bread crumbs by running chunks of it through a food processor or blender to then be added to meatloaf or stuffing or other such instances where bread crumbs are required, but the only real response to such speculation in light of the described bread pudding is simply why?

Nothing need be wasted. There is always some purpose the thing can be used for, a truth as important to bread-making errors as to our own spiritual lives. Nothing is wasted. Nothing is without purpose. Nothing cannot be redeemed.

From the beginning of this book we have been journeying from the significance of the Incarnation toward what it means for our daily lives, seeking what Jesus would have us know about who we are, about the world, about each other, about how he is made known to us. Thousands of years ago in a manger, the creator of all came into the midst of us, said that he would be made known to us as we ourselves are known to each other. In Bethlehem, the House of Bread, the bread of heaven came down to us, and in coming down to us he fed us, and in feeding us he sent us out into the world, out of the House of Bread, to feed the world from the table he prepared, to bring back those who are willing to meet him themselves.

I heard a story once.

A group of children at a church were being instructed in the Liturgy of the Light, a catechetical practice in the season of Easter, in which the young ones are reminded that although Jesus has died, Jesus has also risen, and we are called to share the light of the risen Jesus with the world. The paschal candle, a white pillar lit during the Easter season to symbolize the resurrected Jesus, is placed on a table the children can reach, and after a few brief readings from Scripture and reminding of what Easter means for the church and for each of them, they are invited by name to come forward, take a white candle of their own and light it with the light of the paschal candle, to symbolize to them how the risen Jesus is not just risen but is risen and now makes his light shine in them. Traditionally, the children are called one by one by name to receive the light, but on this particular Sunday there was a visiting child the instructors didn't know. Somehow his name had been missed, and as each child was called down the line to receive the light of Jesus, they began to wonder what they would do. When it was time for his name to be called, without pause one of the instructors said to him, "I don't know your name, but Jesus, the Good Shepherd, does; would you like to come forward and light your candle?"

And he did.

What does it mean to be a temple of the Holy Spirit? What does it mean that the wisdom of God dwells in us? It is both for us and not for us, both so that we may be caught up into the life of God and that we may show others that they can be as well. We are sent forth to not return alone.

"I don't know your name, but Jesus, the Good Shepherd, does; would you like to come forward and light your candle?"

Again and again and again.

I am packing up the sixth kitchen when I receive the news Barbara has passed. My spiritual director departed this life in God's faith and fear while I picked months-forgotten grains of rice from the backs of cupboards. It is nearly midnight, but the season is turning, and deep indigo sets the night sky, impossibly holding light even at this hour. I put on shoes and head out into the blue, make a few turns and find myself on the path. There is only one streetlamp on it, near a corner where the path splits. It glows bright in the evening, flickers, and I think of Barbara as flickering free, a light caught up into the life of God now more fully than I can understand.

I stand in the blue and watch the light, unsure of whether to walk a bit of the path or not. Grief has not visited my heart yet, because when someone dies well it seems to hold back a few hours so the good death can be savored. Barbara walked the path eight decades, circled it back and forth, took side roads and offshoots, and at long last journeyed to the final Feast. The blue, like the metaphorical waters of God we are caught within, swimming about as God saturates this world, seems endless. The sky is full of God's unwavering reminder that all is hid in God, all is made whole in God.

It is the season in which Barbara dies; it is the season in which I pack up a kitchen. We live our lives together and separate, plural and singular, and our seasons overlap, mingle, merge. All of it, every last bit of it, not lost to God. The Good Shepherd is here, right here, even when the answers do not come and the seasons seem long. The Good Shepherd remains. Maybe he doesn't always give an answer, but he shows up. Endless blue in the middle of the night. He shows up.

It seems like an endpoint, but it's not. What happens now is you go make a table and notice who is not invited; you abstain from something for a time to keep mindful of our need for God; you consider the ways in which ordinary things point back to Jesus; you sit in the words of those gone before us in the faith; you marvel at the fullness of the creation; you pray fierce and sure because God hears; you love the Scripture that shows you the face of God; you find the peace within you the Spirit longs for you to know.

And you take a moment to look back at the season of life you have just journeyed, to consider it, to love it for what it is and what it was. You look back just long enough to keep yourself mindful of what it means to move forward. You look back long enough to see if anyone was left behind. Then you keep on the path once more. Then you keep in mind the story you'll hand down like the command in Deuteronomy 6, to the ones who come after you, to the ones who will ask about the seasons and the rhythms and the changes in the path. You'll keep in the mind the story of you, the story of us, the story of Jesus. Tangled, rooted, held. How we leave the House of Bread to return to it. How we are telling the same stories over and over, how the retelling teaches us something new each time about what it means to be fed, what it means to be full.

This week, practice the discipline of recognizing the seasons. This is a similar practice to the Examen, but it concerns itself with a longer period of time than just a day. Consider the last several weeks, the months, the movement in you as you journeyed this book, and take time to inquire of the Spirit what it is you have learned, struggled with, enjoyed. Keep a written record if you're inclined, and I do encourage you to. A check-in with yourself and with the Spirit within you every handful of months is a gift, a gift that helps you see how you have both come to know yourself and God better. Consider the disciplines you engaged, the struggles and the triumphs, and think critically about what was revealed to you or confirmed. As I mentioned there is likely a discipline you very much did not enjoy. Take some time to consider why. But there was likely something you very much did enjoy, and it is worth considering why as well.

Invite the Spirit to guide your thoughts, to show you the places where there is more work to be done, where you may be led next. It is possible that *lectio divina* was a great challenge and one you were grateful to be done with, but the Spirit prompts you to return to it for a season. Don't resist the impulse, for what God may be seeking to work in you is likely more marvelous and good than you could ever imagine, so lean into the impulse and seek where God may take you. Consider too how your understanding of God's presence and the process of discernment has grown in the past weeks, if something new is at work in you. This time of reflection should be a joyous one, and if you find yourself being critical because you missed a week here and there or skipped over this or that, do not ignore this voice of negativity, but give it immediately to the power of Jesus. Only the Accuser condemns the children of God as not being enough. This is not the voice of Jesus; this is not the voice of the Good Shepherd, who knows your name.

The Good Shepherd says he loves you. The Good Shepherd says you are enough. The Good Shepherd delights in every last inch of progress made along the path, for the path is hid in him and every movement is never wasted, never lost, never in vain.

You are a temple of the Holy Spirit. You are caught up in the very life of God. Today, right now, and for all time.

For This Week

DISCIPLINE

- Take time this week to reflect on the last several weeks of disciplines and practices. Consider what you enjoyed and what you did not, what you still have questions about or perhaps what at first you didn't enjoy but have come to appreciate. Write these things down and keep them safe so you can return to them in the future to note how you have changed your mind, stayed the same.

- Make a commitment to incorporate some of the disciplines—perhaps the Examen or the contemplation of icons—and into the season of life you find yourself in. Consider inviting others to join you in the practice, to journey the path together for a time.

- Plan a day about six months from now to check in with yourself again, evaluate where you have been over the weeks and what God has been showing you, teaching you, leading you in.

BAKE

- While not specific to baking per se, clean your oven if it's not something you normally do, following the directions on pages 153–54.

- Do a bit of research and put your leftover bread to good use. Try a bread pudding or make croutons. Notice the ways in which you can ensure nothing is wasted from the effort or the making of the bread.

- Consider branching out into new territory, trying new kinds of bread and baked things. You have honed your skills for weeks now and you're well on your way to mastering all kinds of delights in the future. Take the risk and try your hand at something new. But return to the common bread when you need to, both to remember and to center yourself.

ASK

- In what ways do the disciplines focus you on God? Do you find yourself drawn to particular practices because of personality or seasons of life?

- What are some of the things God has revealed to you or confirmed to you over the course of these past weeks? What feels new in you? What feels strengthened?

- What was the discipline you enjoyed the most over the course of this book? What was the discipline you enjoyed the least? Why? Can you see yourself returning to the discipline you disliked in the future?

Commissioning

I have lived in six kitchens. Actually, at the time of this writing, it's now seven.

We are, you and I, on the path but unsure of the distance, though we have some certainty about where we have come from and where we are going. It occurred to me that saying, "I'm on the path," may be the truest confession of my faith. But it occurs to me that saying, "We're on the path," is a good deal more encouraging, more truthful, more strengthening.

It is stripped of all self-reliance, of all surety but this: we are walking forward; we are walking toward. And when one of us is not, someone will turn around. Someone will go back. Someone will pick us up. Someone will. Someone.

We are all, at some point, someone's someone.

That's the beauty of it. The impossibility of it. The confession of being a temple of the Holy Spirit.

We are the image and likeness of Someone.

And we've come through several weeks together, we've baked some bread, and we've prayed some prayers. There will still be questions and seasons of drought. There will still be burnt bread and overproofed dough. But those are concerns for another day, another season, another year. What comes now is your own. I'm not sure there remains anything else but to say this:

Journey on, you whose name is known to the Good Shepherd, you who are made in the image and likeness of him. Journey on.

With the expectation of the season, with gratitude for the ways in which you make the name of God known, however you make it known,

PRESTON,
CHRISTMAS EVE, 2014

Appendix 1

Suggested Resources for the Tradition

⟫⟫⟫ ⟪⟪⟪

Places to Begin Study (an eclectic list, to start)

- *The Imitation of Christ* by Thomas à Kempis

- *The Interior Castle* by Teresa of Ávila

- *The Life of Moses* by Gregory of Nyssa

- *A Year with the Church Fathers*, edited by Mike Aquilina

- *The Wounded Heart of God: The Asian Concept of Han and the Christian Doctrine of Sin* by Andrew S. Park

- *The Cross and the Lynching Tree* by James H. Cone

- *The Complete Stories* by Flannery O'Connor

- *The Power and the Glory* by Graham Greene

- *Prayers from the Ark and the Creatures' Choir* by Carmen Bernos de Gasztold

- *Luke* by David Lyle Jeffrey for the Brazos Theological Commentary Series

More on the Church Year

- *The Liturgical Year: The Spiraling Adventure of the Spiritual Life — The Ancient Practices Series* by Joan Chittister

- *Living the Christian Year: Time to Inhabit the Story of God* by Bobby Gross

- *To Crown the Year: Decorating the Church through the Seasons* by Peter Mazar

More on Fixed-Hour Prayer

- The series *The Divine Hours* by Phyllis Tickle

- *The Little Book of Hours: Praying With the Community of Jesus* by the Community of Jesus

- *Seven Sacred Pauses: Living Mindfully Through the Hours of the Day* by Macrina Wiederkehr

- *A Book of Hours* by Thomas Merton

- *Common Prayer: A Liturgy for Ordinary Radicals* by Shane Claiborne, Jonathan Wilson-Hartgrove, and Enuma Okoro

Appendix 2

Suggested Resources for Contemplating Icons

These icons, traditional and nontraditional, are easy to come by doing a quick Google search, though it is best to specify with the word *icon* after the traditional works in order to ensure the proper results. A short list of suggestions, to get you started.

TRADITIONAL

- Andrei Rublev Trinity (Ask: What does the conversation within God sound like?)

- Our Lady of the Sign, or the Platytéra (Ask: What does it mean to bear Christ within me?)

- The Presentation of Our Lord (Ask: What does it mean to expect Jesus?)

- Baptism of Our Lord (Ask: What does Jesus do in the waters for us?)

- Crucifixion of Our Lord (Ask: What does it mean that God died?)

- Resurrection of Our Lord (Ask: What does the resurrection mean today and eternally?)

- Ascension of Our Lord (Ask: What has Jesus given us to do now?)

- Pentecost (Ask: To whom have I been sent?)

NONTRADITIONAL, CONCRETE

- *Exodus* by Marc Chagall, 1966 (Ask: Where is God in the Exodus?)

- *Jésus Sera En Agonie Jusqu'a La Fin Du Monde* ["Jesus will be in agony until the end of the world"] by Georges Rouault, 1948 (Ask: What does the suffering of Jesus do then and now?)

- *The Birth of Jesus Christ* by Woonbo Kim Ki-chang, 1953 (Ask: To who and for whom did Jesus come?)

- *He is Risen* by He Qi (Ask: Where has Jesus gone?)

- *Bathsheba at Her Bath* by Rembrandt, 1654 (Ask: What does her face say to me?)

- *By Faith, Not by Sight* by Alix Beaujour (Ask: Who do I say Jesus is?)

- *The Raising of Lazarus* by Van Gogh, 1890 (Ask: What is the surprise of returning to life?)

NONTRADITIONAL, ABSTRACT

- *Golden Fire II* by Makoto Fujimura (Ask: How does the Spirit come to me?)

- *All About the Ladder* by Mollie Walker Freeman (Ask: What is heaven like?)

- *Convergence* by Jackson Pollock, 1952 (Ask: What is the struggle of the light and dark?)

- *Deep Field: Spiral Galaxy 1* by Gareth Bate (Ask: What is human that God should think of us?)

- *He Reigns Supreme Forever II* by Ruth Palmer (Ask: Is the field Jesus planted within me ready to grow and harvest?)

- *Irish Blessing* by Michel Keck (Ask: How does God come to meet me?)

- *City of Light* by Luiza Vizoli, 2010 (Ask: Where does God dwell?)

Acknowledgments

Thank you to my wife, Hilary, for whom words fail and an ocean of meaning is bounded by the promise "okay." Thank you to our best friends, Sam and Chérie Pomeroy, who prove that neither depths nor heights can separate people who love in the way God loves. Thank you to Grant Shellhouse, who is still the best person to sit in a car and talk to. Thank you to my parents, Roger and Pauline, for the unwavering conviction of their faith, their love, and their hope.

Thank you to Shauna Niequist for writing the foreword and for not thinking I was crazy when I asked, for being a modern pioneer in conversations about ordinary life in sacramental spaces, and for these words, which forever changed how I write: "Do your thing with great love."

Thank you to HopePointe Anglican Church for providing me with an incredible year to teach, study, and work on this book in community. Thank you to Bishop Clark Lowenfield for giving me a job and for being the finest example, other than my father, of biblical shepherding and direction. Thank you to Deacon Lisa Schwandt, Canon Steven Saul, Sandy Rambach, Jessica Wilson, and everyone on HopePointe staff for their wit and wisdom and for their prayers and support.

I could not have done any of this without my agent, John Topliff, and his wife, Debby, who beyond being supports and tireless advocates for my work have loved our family well. They are lights in a land of lingering shadows.

This is the book I didn't know I had always wanted to write until I was given the permission to write it. That permission and subsequent challenge, encouragement, and direction came from my extraordinary editor, John Sloan, to whom I remain eternally grateful for telling me *no* or *more here* or *What does this even mean?* Bob Hudson, my copyeditor, has saved this book and the one before it from making a fool of itself, and is one of the kindest wielders of the editorial pen I know. Alicia, Jennifer, Carolyn, Stephanie, and Bridget have in no small way been champions of projects I only dreamed I would get to create. All of these extraordinary people are what make Zondervan the most welcoming place to publish and a press that deeply loves God and God's kingdom.

Thank you to Nish Weiseth, who reminds me to do the hard thing because it's the better thing. Thank you to Seth Haines, Chad Markley, Mike Rusch, and Troy Livesay for being daily sources of laughter and insight. Thank you to Ralph Wood for reminding me to write less *about* and more *of* me; to David Jeffrey for classes on the Bible and Christian faith that have remained with me and continue to challenge me. Thank you to Sarah Bessey, Rachel Held Evans, Deidra Riggs, Kathy Khang, Alia Joy Hagenbach, Mark and Kristen Howerton, Jennifer Dukes Lee, and Tsh Oxenreider for the counsel, admonishment, and generous words.

Thank you to three semesters of Sacramental Baking participants, for their patience and generosity and willingness to muddle through and work through and test out so much of what became the contents of this book. They are a gift, each and every one, and wherever we all find ourselves on the path, they are in the midst of doing a great work. Thank you to Elora Ramirez, for giving me the chance to first try out teaching the class and helping me dream big.

Finally, thank you to our Good Shepherd. May this be a work of honoring the One unto whom all things shall tend in their time.

Notes

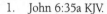

1. John 6:35a KJV.

2. 1 Corinthians 6:19 ESV.

3. As quoted in *The Catechism of the Catholic Church* Part 1.460, Catholic Church. Catechism of the Catholic Church. 2nd ed. Vatican: Libreria Editrice Vaticana, 2000, 129.

4. Bishop Kallistos Ware, *The Orthodox Way* (Crestwood: St. Vladmir's Seminary Press, 1995), 125.

5. Genesis 1:26 KJV.

6. Origen, *On First Principles* III, vi, 1, tr. G.W. Butterworth (London: SPCK, 1936), 245.

7. Exodus 31:1–11 ESV.

8. Though the ESV translation uses *men*, it is used in the sense of *humankind*, men and women alike were called by God for this task, which is confirmed to us throughout Exodus 31–36.

9. Deuteronomy 12:11 ESV.

10. See Exodus 35:11, 35:35, 36:1. 36:8.

11. Disagreement exists between Exodus and Deuteronomy on this point. In Exodus 30, the instruction is given to Bezalel and Oholiab; in Deuteronomy 10, Moses builds the ark without reference to anyone else. This is likely because Exodus is a book about establishing how the people relate to God and Deuteronomy a book about the Law, establishing Moses as a central figure of the faith.

12. 1 Kings 3:2–14 ESV.

13. Divrei Hayamim II–II Chronicles–Chapter 1.

14. Wisdom of Solomon 9 NRSV.

15. John 1:13–16 ESV.

16. 1 Corinthians 1:23b–24 ESV.

17. 1 Corinthians 11:28–31 ESV.

18. Romans 8:26 ESV.

19. 1 John 4:1 ESV.

20. Matthew 4:3 NASB.

21. Matthew 4:4 NASB.

22. Matthew 4:5–6 NASB.

23. Matthew 4:7 NASB.

24. Luke 4:16–21 NASB.

25. Krista Tippet (host) and Lawrence Kushner (guest). (2014, May 15). *On Being* [Audio podcast]. Retrieved from http://www.onbeing.org/program/lawrence-kushner-kabbalah-and-the-inner-life-of-god/6309.

26. Psalm 22:3 ESV.

27. Romans 10:8–10 ESV.

28. *Walking on Water*, 38.

29. Acts 1:9 ESV.

30. Ephesians 2:18 ESV.

31. Luke 18:1–8 NRSV.

32. A paraphrase of Ecclesiastes 3:11.

33. "How Gentle God's Commands" by Philip Doddridge.

34. Charles Tomlinson, "Eden."

35. Simone Weil, *Waiting for God* (New York: HarperCollins, 2009), 8.

36. John 6:51 NRSV.

37. Saint Gregory of Nyssa, *On the Baptism of Christ*.

38. See John 20.

39. Saint Cyril of Jerusalem, *Catechetical Lecture 15*.

40. Romans 8:19–21 ESV.

41. David Bentley Hart, *The Beauty of the Infinite* (Grand Rapids: Eerdmans, 2003), 187.

42. Acts 17:28 ESV.

43. 2 Peter 3:9 ESV.

44. 1 Corinthians 4:7 NASB.

45. Deuteronomy 6:6–9 ESV.

46. Paraphrase of Philippians 2:12.

47. Genesis 12:6 ESV.

48. John 4:20 ESV.

49. John 4:21–24 ESV.

50. Colossians 1:15 ESV.

51. Luke 1:38 KJV.

52. Saint Augustine, *De Doctrina Christiana* 40, 60.

53. Malachi 4:2 ESV.

54. Matthew 6:16–19 ESV.

55. Romans 6:3–5 ESV.

56. Isaiah 9:2 ESV.

57. Acts 2:42 ESV.

58. Genesis 1:2 ESV.

59. See Colossians 1:16.

60. John 6:35 ESV.

61. John 6:48–51 ESV.

62. John 6:53–59 ESV.

63. John 6:68–69 ESV.

64. Luke 24:30–33, 35 ESV.

65. 1 Corinthians 11:27, 30 ESV.

66. Matthew 18:20 ESV.

67. John 4:29 NLT.

68. John 10:10 ESV.

69. John 6:37 ESV.